Chef Charlotte

AMIGURUMI DRESS-UP DOLL
WITH TEA PARTY PLAY SET

Chef Charlotte

Amigurumi Dress-Up Doll with Tea Party Play Set

Crochet Patterns for 12" Doll plus Doll Clothes, Oven, Pastries, Tablecloth and Accessories

Linda Wright

In memory of my cat, Cookie

Also by Linda Wright

Honey Bunny Amigurumi Dress Up-Doll with Garden Play Mat
Honey Pie Amigurumi Dress-Up Doll with Picnic Play Set
Amigurumi Christmas Ornaments
Amigurumi Golf Club Covers
Amigurumi Toilet Paper Covers
Amigurumi Animal Hats
Amigurumi Animal Hats Growing Up
Amigurumi Animal Hats for 18-Inch Dolls
Amigurumi Holiday Hats for 18-Inch Dolls
Toilet Paper Origami
Toilet Paper Origami On a Roll

Credits
Photography: Linda and Randy Wright

All rights reserved. Permission is granted to copy or reprint portions for any noncommercial use, except they may not be posted online without permission. You may sell the finished products that you make yourself at your local bazaar, craft fair, etc. but not on the internet. Items cannot be mass produced without the publisher's written permission. Contact the publisher with licensing inquiries.

Copyright © 2021 Linda Wright
Edition 1.0

Lindaloo Enterprises
P.O. Box 90135
Santa Barbara, California 93190
United States
sales@lindaloo.com

ISBN: 978-1-937564-16-2
Library of Congress Control Number: 2021919701

CONTENTS

GETTING STARTED

Introduction	8
Supplies	10
Abbreviations	13
Gauge	13
How to Read a Pattern	13

DOLL

Charlotte	14

WARDROBE

Chef Dress	18
Chef Dress Variations	19
Chef Uniform	20
Half Apron	23
Oven Mitts	23
Full Apron	24
Cupcake Blouse	25
Pleated Skirt	26
Boatneck Tunic	27
Tulip Pants	29
Chocolate Chip Cookie Purse	30
Confetti Donut Purse	31
Tea Party Purse	32
Tea Party Hat	33
Stole	34
Lace Nightgown	35
Mary Janes	36
Chef Shoes	36
Sprinkle Slippers	37
Booties	37

TEA PARTY

Tablecloth	38

Accessories

Tea Pot	39
Teaspoon	40
Fork	41
Knife	41
Cream Pitcher	42
Sugar Bowl	43
Tea Cup & Saucer	44
Tea Napkin	45
Napkin Ring	45
Party Plate	46
Serving Plate	47
2-Tier Pastry Plate	48
1-Tier Pastry Plate	49
Vase of Flowers	50

How to Set the Table	51

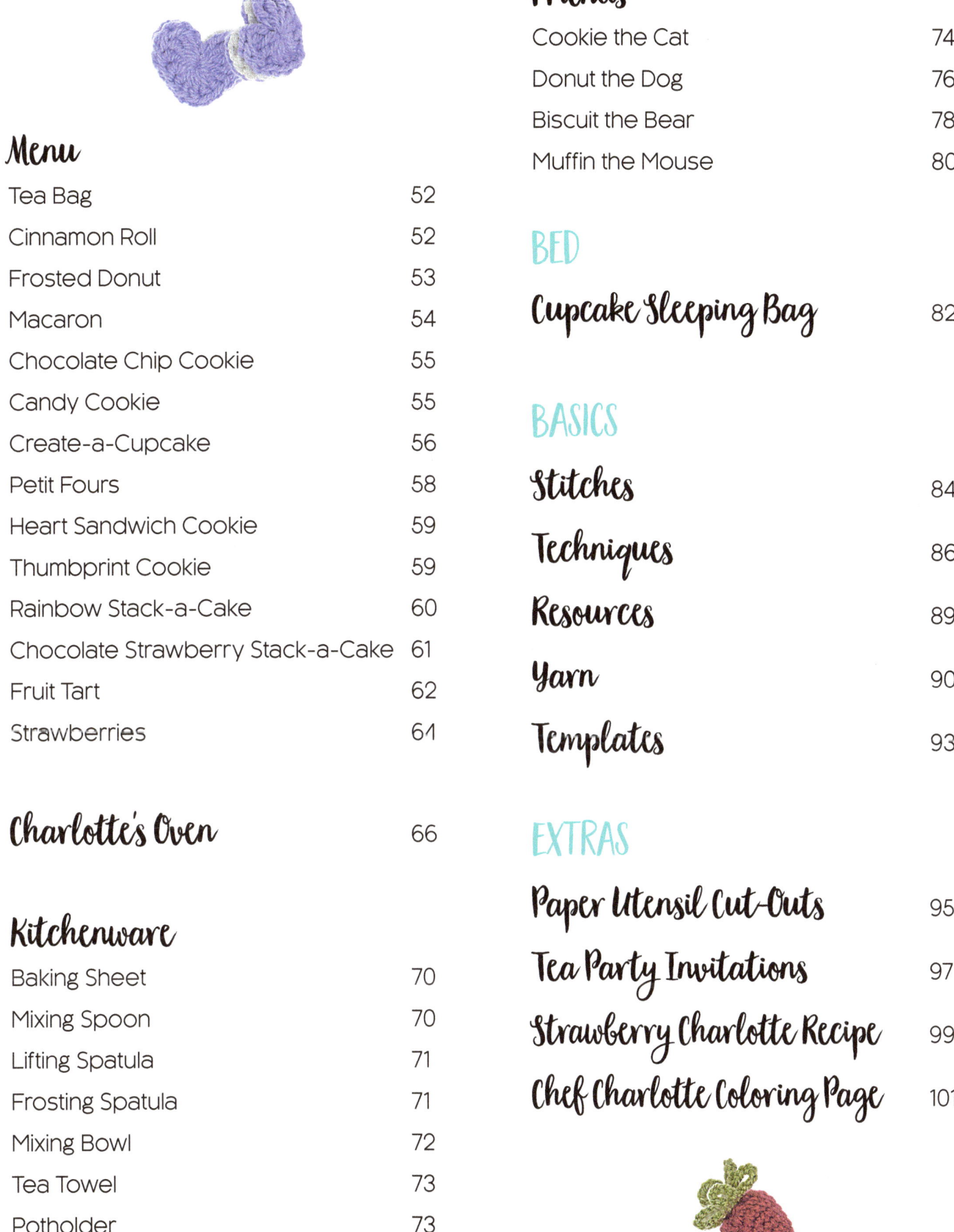

Menu

Tea Bag	52
Cinnamon Roll	52
Frosted Donut	53
Macaron	54
Chocolate Chip Cookie	55
Candy Cookie	55
Create-a-Cupcake	56
Petit Fours	58
Heart Sandwich Cookie	59
Thumbprint Cookie	59
Rainbow Stack-a-Cake	60
Chocolate Strawberry Stack-a-Cake	61
Fruit Tart	62
Strawberries	64

Charlotte's Oven 66

Kitchenware

Baking Sheet	70
Mixing Spoon	70
Lifting Spatula	71
Frosting Spatula	71
Mixing Bowl	72
Tea Towel	73
Potholder	73

Friends

Cookie the Cat	74
Donut the Dog	76
Biscuit the Bear	78
Muffin the Mouse	80

BED

Cupcake Sleeping Bag 82

BASICS

Stitches	84
Techniques	86
Resources	89
Yarn	90
Templates	93

EXTRAS

Paper Utensil Cut-Outs	95
Tea Party Invitations	97
Strawberry Charlotte Recipe	99
Chef Charlotte Coloring Page	101

INTRODUCTION

Chef Charlotte is a pastry-chef doll who is every bit as sweet as the goodies she bakes! Charlotte thrives on hosting charming Tea Parties with pretty trimmings. She loves her colorful oven, sprinkles, anything pink and everything cupcake. She has cupcake slippers, a cupcake purse, cupcake sleeping bag and, of course, cupcakes to eat!

In this book, you will find crochet patterns for a 12-inch Charlotte doll, her clothes, oven and a complete Tea Party Play Set. Party guests include Donut the Dog, Cookie the Cat, Biscuit the Bear and Muffin the Mouse. That frisky foursome is always eager to tell tales of their adventures over tea! You will also make a tablecloth big enough to set the table for all of the dolls — plus the necessary accessories for a perfect tea party.

These patterns were designed for play, not just display. Little chefs can mix imaginary batter, bake amigurumi pastries, frost them and assemble them on serving plates. They can steep tea, build towering cakes and create magical cupcakes with frosting that pops into place with magnets.

Mini sets of silverware will help children learn how to set the table — and enable the dolls to properly eat their cake. Besides flatware to crochet, 4 place settings of silverware are provided as paper cut-outs (see page 95). When the page is backed with thin cardboard and laminated with package tape before cutting, the utensils are stiff, shiny and durable.

Charlotte's wardrobe includes workwear, everyday wear, partywear and sleepwear. Her lacy nightgown is made with a lovely shell stitch. Please note that when you dress your doll, her clothes are designed to slide on feet-first.

Before starting, be sure to read through the next 5 introductory pages plus the Stitches and Techniques sections at the back of the book. You will find essential information. If you're new to crocheting and like to learn by watching, YouTube.com offers a treasure trove of excellent crocheting tutorials. These are also great for experienced crocheters who need to brush up. I have assembled a collection of my favorite videos on Pinterest. You can view them at www.pinterest.com/LindalooEnt/ on a board named "Amigurumi Tutorials".

Amigurumi is a specific type of crochet for making 3D objects and toys. It primarily uses easy single crochet stitches for an even surface. Stuffing brings the amigurumi to life. Many amigurumi patterns are worked in the round as a continuous spiral. I like to start these with a Magic Ring, but you can replace the ring with a simple 'chain 2'; then work the specified stitches in the 2nd chain from the hook instead of the ring. To read more about this, see page 86.

I had great fun using beads in these patterns. Bugle beads create shimmery sprinkles on garments and goodies. Seed beads are used on some of the food. Embroidery can be substituted if desired.

Charlotte is a soft doll with legs that rotate for sitting. Her arms are unstuffed and flexible. If you want to make a rigid doll that can hold a pose, wire can be added inside the arms, legs or both. (See "Adding Wire" on page 88.)

I strive to write my patterns with easy techniques and clear instructions so they will be fun and rewarding for crocheters of any level. In this book, here are a few of the things I'm especially excited to show you how to make:

- movable thread-jointed legs
- a delightful 2-tier pastry plate
- magnetic mix-and-match cupcakes
- 2 fabulous stack-a-cakes
- a fun-for-play oven
- and, Charlotte's super-cute and easy hairstyle!

This book uses U.S. crochet terms. If an instruction says sc, that is a U.S. single crochet — or a U.K. double crochet. Please refer to the stitch diagrams at the back of the book to be sure you are making the stitches as intended.

Chef Charlotte is a companion to my previous dress-up dolls with themed play sets: **Honey Bunny** includes a delightful plant-and-pick garden. **Honey Pie** features a barbecue play mat with a picnic play set. The 3 dolls are similar enough in size to be perfect playmates. They can share accessories and many of their clothes.

I have tucked a few surprises into the back of this book. First is the set of silverware cut-outs previously mentioned. Next is a recipe for a charlotte. A charlotte is a type of fancy dessert, so it only seemed fitting to include a recipe for Chef Charlotte's namesake cake. My kid-friendly version features a vessel of Twinkies® that holds a strawberry whipped-cream filling. Next I've included Tea Party invitations for inviting your guests. Finally, you'll find a coloring page that is fun for all ages!

May you and the children in your life have hours of fun hosting tea parties with Chef Charlotte. If you enjoy my book, I would appreciate it so much if you leave a review at your online place of purchase. Other customers would appreciate it too!

Now gather up your crochet hooks — and get ready to capture the essence of afternoon tea with amigurumi!

 Linda

Supplies

Yarn

These projects have been made with acrylic yarns that are readily available and inexpensive. Worsted-weight yarn (#4) is used for items that need a sturdy structure. DK/Light Worsted (#3) is used for items that have a more delicate nature or that need to drape. My go-to #3 yarn is Stylecraft "Special DK" from lovecrafts.com. It comes in a fantastic range of colors at an excellent price. Be sure to check each pattern in this book for its yarn weight specification. The specific yarns I used are listed on pages 90-91.

Crochet Hooks

The following hooks are used: C2/2.75mm, D3/3.25mm, E4/3.5mm, F5/3.75mm, G6/4mm and H8/5mm.

My favorite hook is the Clover Soft Touch. I love the thick handle and the shape of the head which inserts easily into a stitch.

Ruler

For measuring and marking.

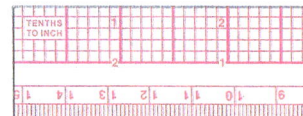

Yarn Needle

You will need a large-eyed needle to sew the various pieces of your items together and also to finish them off by weaving the loose ends into your work. Yarn needles with a blunt point are readily available but I frequently like to use a one with a sharp point. These can be hard to find in stores, so if you'd like one, plan to shop online. My favorite is the Size 14 Chenille or Embroidery needle.

Stitch Markers

Stitch markers are used to keep track of where a round or row of crochet begins and ends. You can use a bobby pin, safety pin or purchased stitch markers. You can also use a scrap of yarn (see page 87). Making the correct number of stitches is important, so count to double check if ever you're not sure.

Scissors

You will need a small pair of sharp scissors.

Safety Eyes

Plastic safety eyes give amigurumi a professional look. Each eye has a post section and a washer. To attach with washer, work post into a gap between stitches, place washer against post, lay eye against a hard surface and press washer firmly. Eyes can also be attached with glue, omitting the washer.

Plastic safety eyes contain small parts. If the doll is for a child under age 3, I recommend using embroidery or small felt circles as alternatives.

Sewing Needle & Thread

If you don't have a supply of thread, one spool of clear nylon thread, called "invisible thread", will match everything.

Straight Pins

Use ball head dressmaker's pins or long corsage pins to hold pieces in place before sewing.

Row Counter

Well worth the investment, a row counter keeps track of what round or row of the pattern you are crocheting. A pencil and paper can also be used. Crochet apps for mobile devices are available too. A simple Android app that I like is called Minimalist Stitch Counter.

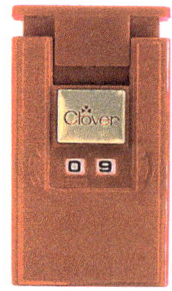

Removable Notes

Use small sticky notes to keep track of your place in a pattern. Every time you complete a round or a row, move the note down to reveal the next line of instructions. I wouldn't work without one!

Stuffing & Stuffing Tools

Polyester fiberfill, or polyfill, is the best stuffing material. Yarn scraps can be used for stuffing very small pieces. The eraser end of a new pencil, a blunt-tipped chopstick or tweezers make great stuffing tools. I highly recommend a pair of 6-inch straight-tip serrated tweezers. I find them invaluable for inserting stuffing through small openings.

Glue

Glue is used for some of the assembly. Be sure to choose glues that dry clear. **Fast Grab Tacky Glue** and **Gem-Tac** are great for attaching plastic embellishments such as eyes and beads. **Fabri-Tac** is wonderful for joining fabric to fabric. Use **Super Glue** or **Glue Dots** for magnets and washers. **Tacky Glue, Elmer's Glue-All** and **Hot Glue** are good all-purpose choices. With any glue, I recommend practicing with scraps before working on your actual project to become familiar with how the glue reacts. If using hot glue, you will want to know how to prevent the formation of messy strings. Video demos of various methods are available on YouTube. **Tip:** release trigger of glue gun and move tip in small rapid circles to break string before pulling gun away from your work.

Beads

Beads elevate the look of amigurumi and bring an element of bling. I buy them at craft stores, Amazon and Etsy. They can be attached with glue or sewing. If you choose to sew them on, you will need a beading needle. Beading needles are thin and flexible. Some have large collapsible eyes; others have very small eyes that will require a needle-threader for threading.

To attach beads with glue, bent-nose tweezers are the key to ease. Squeeze some glue on a scrap of foil or paper. Grip bead with tweezers, dip lightly in glue, drop in place on crochet, and tap with your finger to press bead into fabric.

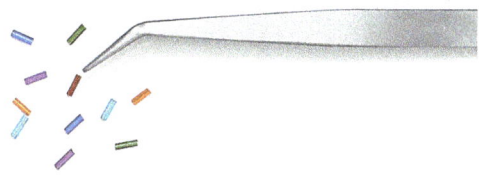

Embroidery can be substituted for beads, if desired. At the very least, I recommend getting a package of 6mm multi-color bugle beads. They are used for multiple patterns and they add so much pizazz!

Magnets

Magnets are an exciting way to make your amigurumi more dynamic. The neodymium magnets used in this book have a very strong pull when they are bare. To separate them, slide — don't pull. When encased in crochet, the attraction is weakened and they will be easy for children to pull apart.

Magnets are attached to the crochet with glue. My recommendations are provided in the Glue section on this page. Note: Hot glue should not be used on neodymium magnets as the heat can demagnetize them.

Marking your Magnets: In order to attract, the opposite poles of 2 magnets must meet. Many bulk magnets are not labeled for their poles (north and south). You can simply play with a pair to see how they need to face in order to stick — but I like to mark them in advance: Using a pen that will write on metal (e.g. Sharpie), take your stack of magnets and mark all same-facing sides with an "X". This makes it easy to identify poles that are the same.

Fun Fact: Magnets can be stacked to increase their strength.

Abbreviations

The following abbreviations are used:

yd = yard

st = stitch

ch = chain

sc = single crochet

hdc = half double crochet

dc = double crochet

sl st = slip stitch

rnd = round

invdec = invisible decrease

sc2tog = single crochet 2 stitches together

sc3tog = single crochet 3 stitches together

* * = a set of stitches; repeat instructions between asterisks as many times as directed

( ) = stitch count; also indicates a group of sts worked together in the same stitch or space

Gauge

Gauge is a measure of how big your stitches are. It's very common for gauge to vary from person-to-person because not all crocheters stitch the same way. Yarn selection also affects gauge. Some yarns are thinner than others despite being in the same weight category.

Gauge is not critical in these projects. The main thing is to have the doll clothes fit your doll. Have fittings before the garments are done and make adjustments if needed.

To alter your gauge, adjust your crochet tension (tightness); change to a larger or smaller crochet hook; try a different brand of hook; or try a different brand of yarn.

The following gauge is used in these patterns.

With **G6/4mm hook** and **DK, Light Worsted yarn**:

21 sc = 4"; 23 rows = 4"

With **G6/4mm hook** and **Worsted Weight yarn**:

19 sc = 4"; 22 rows = 4"

How to Read a Pattern

Each round or row is written on a new line. Most rounds have a repeated section of instructions that are written between two asterisks *like this*. The instruction between the asterisks is to be repeated as many times as indicated before you move on to the next step. At the end of a round, the total number of stitches to be made in that round is indicated in parentheses (like this).

Let's look at a round.

Rnd 6: *sc in next 4 sts, 2 sc in next st* 6 times (36 sts).

This means:

Rnd 6	This is the 6th round of the pattern.
sc in next 4 sts	Make 1 single crochet stitch in each of the next 4 stitches
2 sc in next st	Make 2 single crochet stitches, both in the same stitch
6 times	Repeat everything between * and * 6 times.
(36 sts)	The round will have a total of 36 stitches.

So, following the instructions for Round 6, you will:

single crochet in the next 4 sts, 2 sc in the next st,

single crochet in the next 4 sts, 2 sc in the next st,

single crochet in the next 4 sts, 2 sc in the next st,

single crochet in the next 4 sts, 2 sc in the next st,

single crochet in the next 4 sts, 2 sc in the next st,

single crochet in the next 4 sts, 2 sc in the next st,

for a total of 36 stitches.

Charlotte

Charlotte is made from worsted-weight yarn. This doll was made with beige skin and brown hair but those features can be customized in any way you wish. You may even want to make her hair pink or purple! Use the same brand of yarn for the doll and hair for the best fit. See page 90 for the specific yarns used here.

The doll parts are crocheted as continuous spirals by working in the round. When crocheting small cylinders such as the arms and legs, a running stitch marker is ideal (see page 87). The eraser end of a new pencil makes a great stuffing tool: by twisting the pencil as you push, the eraser will grab the stuffing nicely. Underwear is created as part of the doll to eliminate the need for an extra layer of bulk under her clothing.

Charlotte's legs are attached by yarn jointing. This is an easy way to make movable legs. If you would like your doll to be able to hold a pose, wire can be added inside. Instructions for this are provided in the Techniques section at the back of the book. Without wire, Charlotte will be soft and cuddly with rotating legs that allow her to sit nicely.

SIZE

12" tall

SUPPLIES

G6/4mm crochet hook

100 yds of Worsted weight yarn in beige

100 yds of Worsted weight yarn in brown

Small amount of Worsted weight yarn in blue

2 black safety eyes, 10mm

Glue (for eyes & fabric, see page 11)

Polyester fiberfill stuffing

HEAD

With beige yarn, make a magic ring, ch 1.

Rnd 1: 6 sc in ring, pull ring closed tight (6 sts).

Rnd 2: 2 sc in each st around. Place marker for beginning of rnd and move marker up as each rnd is completed (12 sts).

Rnd 3: *sc in next st, 2 sc in next st* 6 times (18 sts).

Rnd 4: *sc in next 2 sts, 2 sc in next st* 6 times (24 sts).

Rnd 5: *sc in next 3 sts, 2 sc in next st* 6 times (30 sts).

Rnd 6: *sc in next 4 sts, 2 sc in next st* 6 times (36 sts).

Rnd 7: sc in each st around.

Rnd 8: *sc in next 5 sts, 2 sc in next st* 6 times (42 sts).

Rnds 9-13: sc in each st around.

Note: In Rnds 14-18, sc2tog can be used instead of invdec.

Rnd 14: *sc in next 5 sts, invdec* 6 times (36 sts).

Rnd 15: *sc in next 4 sts, invdec* 6 times (30 sts).

Rnd 16: *sc in next 3 sts, invdec* 6 times (24 sts).

Rnd 17: *sc in next 2 sts, invdec* 6 times (18 sts).

Rnd 18: *sc in next st, invdec* 6 times (12 sts).

Sl st in next st. Fasten off.

BODY

With blue yarn, make a magic ring, ch 1.

Rnd 1: 8 sc in ring, pull ring closed tight (8 sts).

Rnd 2: *sc in next st, 2 sc in next st* 4 times. Place marker for beginning of rnd and move marker up as each rnd is completed (12 sts).

Rnd 3: *sc in next st, 2 sc in next st* 6 times (18 sts).

Rnd 4: *sc in next 2 sts, 2 sc in next st* 6 times (24 sts).

Rnds 5-8: sc in each st around; change to beige yarn in last st of Rnd 8.

Rnds 9-17: sc in each st around.

Rnd 18: *sc in next 2 sts, sc2tog* 6 times (18 sts).

Rnd 19: *sc in next st, sc2tog* 6 times (12 sts).

Sl st in next st. Fasten off.

LEGS (MAKE 2)

With beige yarn, make a magic ring, ch 1.

Rnd 1: 6 sc in ring, pull ring closed tight (6 sts).

Rnd 2: *sc in next st, 2 sc in next st* 3 times. Place marker for beginning of rnd and move marker up as each rnd is completed (9 sts).

Rnds 3-23: sc in each st around.

Rnd 24: for **foot**, 2 sc in next st, 4 sc in next 2 sts, 2 sc in next st, sc in next 6 sts (18 sts).

Rnds 25-26: sc in each st around.

Rnd 27: sc2tog 9 times (9 sts).

Fasten off.

ARMS (MAKE 2)

With beige yarn, make a magic ring, ch 1.

Rnd 1: 9 sc in ring, pull ring closed tight (9 sts).

Rnds 2-3: sc in each st around. Place marker for beginning of rnd and move marker up as each rnd is completed.

Rnd 4: sc2tog twice, sc in next 5 sts (7 sts).

Rnds 5-22: sc in each st around.

Sl st in next st. Fasten off.

ASSEMBLY

Head: Stuff head firmly pushing stuffing outward against surface of sphere to fill out the space. **Stuff until circumference of head is 10" at the widest point so the wig fits.**

Body: Stuff body firmly. Sew head and body together, packing in more stuffing at the neck area for support when seam is nearly closed.

Legs: Stuff the legs. To close hole, thread ending tail onto needle, weave needle in and out around post of each st and pull tight. Hide yarn tails inside legs.

The legs are attached by yarn-jointing. Mark position for legs on each side of body in groove between Rnds 5-6 using a pin or stitch marker (see locations A and B in Fig. X).

Lay body and legs as shown in Fig. X. I used bobby pins to keep the feet facing forward. Cut a generous length of yarn and thread it on a blunt-tipped yarn needle.

1. Push needle into body at A and out at B leaving a tail.

2. Push needle into first leg at C (groove between Rnds 2-3) and out at D.

3. Straddle 2 sts at D, sew back into leg and out in exact same st at C. Be sure the st at D is centered on outer leg so your leg hangs straight.

4. Push needle back in at B and out at A going into exact same sts as before.

5. Push needle into second leg at E (groove between Rnds 2-3) and out at F.

6. Straddle 2 sts at F, sew back into leg and out in exact same st at E. Be sure the st at F is centered on outer leg so your leg hangs straight.

Pull yarn to tighten legs, pulling them into the body a bit. Make sure legs are pulled tight. They will loosen up slightly with time. For extra strength, repeat these steps. Knot yarn ends together and hide tails inside body.

Arms: With eraser end of new pencil, push stuffing into hand only; do not stuff arm. Sew an arm to each side, 1 rnd down from top of body.

Glue **eyes** between Rnds 12-13 with an interspace of 8-9 sts; or mark the locations now but do the final gluing after the hair is done to be sure you like the look.

Embroider **nose** 2 rows below eyes.

Weave in ends.

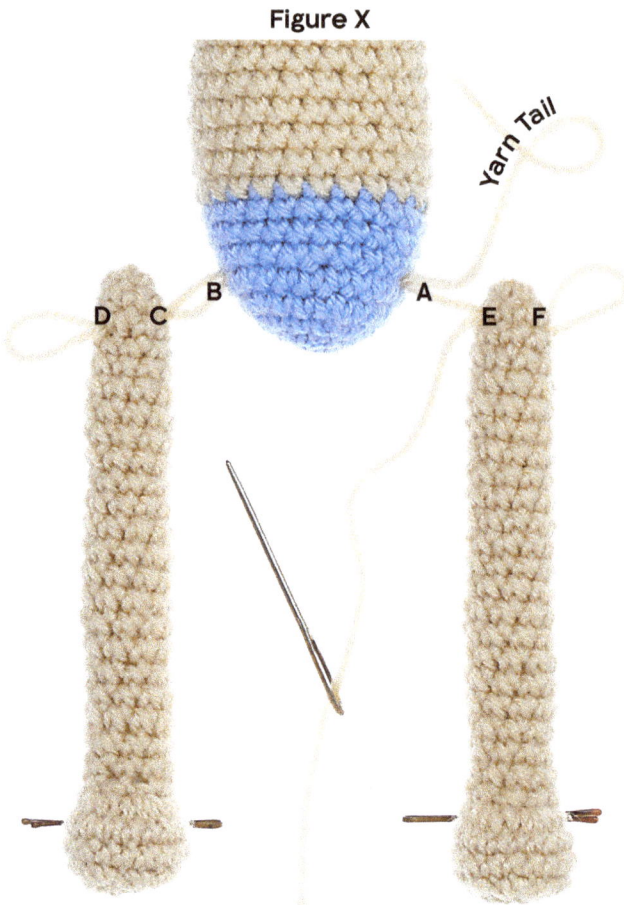

Figure X

Legs are Done

HAIR

Front View   Back View

Note: A chain 1 at the beginning of a row is for turning your work and does not count as a stitch.

WIG BASE

With brown yarn, ch 18.

Row 1: ch 1, turn, sc in each ch across (18 sts).

Row 2: ch 1, turn, working in **back loops only**, sc in each st across.

Row 3: ch 1, turn, resuming work in **both loops**, sc in each st across.

Rows 4-31: repeat Rows 2 and 3.

Measure your work to ensure that it is 7" wide (or 70% of head circumference) and adjust if needed. Refer to photo below. Next the bangs are made.

Row 32: ch 1, turn, working in **back loops only**, sc in next 10 sts (10 sts).

Row 33: ch 1, turn, working in **both loops**, sc in each st across.

Rows 34-45: repeat Rows 32 and 33.

Confirm fit: Strip should be same circumference as head. Adjust if needed to get proper size.

Fasten off with long tail.

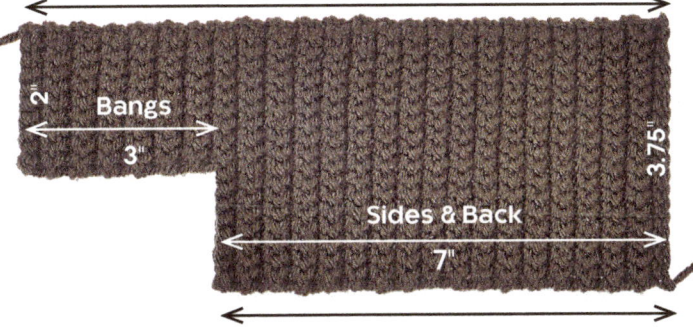

Coil work as shown in Fig. A. Sew 1st & last row together.

Thread a blunt-tipped yarn needle with a generous length of brown yarn. Starting at center back, sew with running stitch around top edge (see Fig. B).

Pull yarn tightly to gather edge, pull closed until a small hole remains (about 1/2", see Fig. C). Secure in place with a knot.

HAIR STRANDS (MAKE 15)

With brown yarn, chain 23.

Row 1: sc in 2nd ch from hook and in each remaining ch across (22 sts). Fasten off with **extra long tail**.

Note: For more volume, you can make more hair strands.

FINISHING

Position hole at top of wig base over Rnd 1 of head and bangs at center front. Attach wig base with sewing or glue. One-by-one, position hair strands over ridges of sides/back portion of wig base and sew tails into hole at top of wig base: stab needle into head and make several sts thru head in different directions to secure the strand. Make these sts in <u>grooves</u> of wig base so they will be hidden. Cut off yarn tails flush with surface.

When all strands are attached, pin them in position with ball-head sewing pins to cover sides/back portion of wig base. Lift each strand gently and glue **upper third** of each strand to wig base. Replace pin until glue dries.

Chef Dress

The Chef Dress was designed with confetti cake in mind! Sprinkles on the skirt make it a sweet dress for a pastry chef. The dress is crocheted from the top down. The work is done in rows to the waistline. This creates an opening at the back. Next, the skirt section is made in continuous rounds. A contrasting color is used for the top section of the skirt to create the look of an apron.

SUPPLIES

G6/4mm crochet hook

Small amount of DK, Light Worsted yarn in pink and white

2 buttons, 3/8" diameter

Bugle beads in assorted colors, 6mm

Glue (for beads, see page 11)

Note: A chain 1 at the beginning of a row is for turning your work and does not count as a stitch.

BODICE

With pink yarn, ch 24.

Row 1: ch 1, turn, sc in each ch across (24 sts).

Row 2: ch 1, turn, sc in next 4 sts; for **armhole**, ch 7 loosely, skip next 3 sts; sc in next 10 sts; for **armhole**, ch 7 loosely, skip next 3 sts; sc in next 4 sts (18 sts, 14 chs).

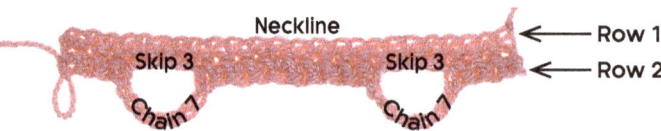

Rows 3-10: ch 1, turn, sc in each st or ch across, join Row 10 with sl st in first st; change to white yarn in the sl st (32 sts).

SKIRT

Now work in rounds.

Rnd 11: 2 dc in each st around. Place marker for beginning of rnd and move marker up as each rnd is completed (64 sts).

Rnd 12: *dc in next st, 2 dc next st* around (96 sts).

Rnds 13-16: dc in each st around.

Rnd 17: working in **front loops only**, dc in each st around.

Sl st in next st. Fasten off. Join pink yarn with sl st in **back loop** of Rnd 16.

Rnd 18: working in **back loops only**, dc in each st around.

Rnds 19-21: resuming work in **both loops**, dc in each st around.

Rnd 22: for **ruffle**, *sc in next st, ch 2* around.

Sl st in next st. Fasten off.

COLLAR

The collar is worked in 2 halves from back corners to center front.

Row 1: join white yarn with sc at left corner, sc in next 11 sts (12 sts).

Row 2: ch 1, turn, *dc in next st, 2 dc in next st* 6 times (18 sts). Fasten off.

Repeat for 2nd half of collar, inserting hook thru **wrong side** of remaining corner.

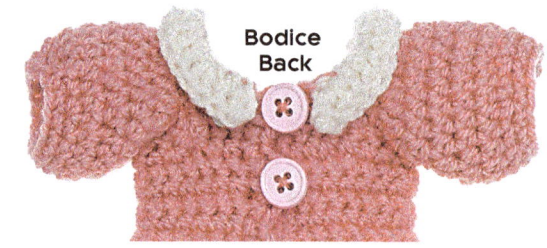

SLEEVES

Join pink yarn anywhere on armhole edge.

Rnd 1: work 14 sc around armhole (14 sts).

Rnd 2: *hdc in next st, 2 hdc in next st* 7 times (21 sts).

Rnds 3-6: hdc in each st around.

Rnd 7: *sc in next st, sc2tog* 7 times (14 sts).

Rnd 8: sc in each st around.

Sl st in next st. Fasten off.

FINISHING

Knot yarn tails together from color change at waistline.

At back opening, the edges are finished with sc. **Button loops** are created as you work: join pink yarn with sc at top right corner of bodice back, sc in next 14 sts; **for 1st button loop,** ch 3, sc in each remaining st until 1 st remains; **for 2nd button loop,** ch 3, sc in last st. Fasten off.

Sew buttons on edge opposite button loops.

Weave in ends.

For **sprinkles,** glue bugle beads to white section of skirt.

Tip: If your dress needs pressed into shape, hang it with clothespins and use a handheld garment steamer.

CHEF DRESS VARIATIONS

The Chef Dress can be transformed into dresses for any occasion by playing with color placement, hem length and embellishments. Use these samples for inspiration! For another look, the collar and sleeves can be omitted.

2 COLORS: Glue bugle beads to bodice.

3 COLORS: The green area creates the look of a pinafore.

1 COLOR: Make a bow of satin ribbon and sew at waist. See page 89 for bow instructions.

4 COLORS: Work collar and ruffle in white. Sew buttons to bodice.

Chef Uniform

Decorative buttons embellish the chef jacket for a double-breasted look. Chef pants are typically made from checkered fabric to hide cooking stains. Multicolor yarn is used here. The hat is the crowning glory of a chef uniform and Charlotte's features a pretty bow.

SUPPLIES

G6/4mm crochet hook

220 yds of DK, Light Worsted yarn in pink

Small amount of DK, Light Worsted yarn in gray & multicolor graytones

Stretch Magic clear elastic bead cord (.7mm)

3 snap fasteners

6 buttons, 5/16" diameter

Sewing thread

Note: A chain 1 at the beginning of a row is for turning your work and does not count as a stitch.

CHEF JACKET

The jacket is worked flat in rows.

FRONT (MAKE 2)

With pink yarn, ch 20.

Rows 1-6: ch 1, turn, sc in each st across (20 sts).

Rows 7-14: ch 1, turn, sc in next 17 sts (17 sts).

Fasten off.

BACK

With pink yarn, ch 20.

Rows 1-6: ch 1, turn, sc in each st across (20 sts).

Rows 7-15: ch 1, turn, sc in next 17 sts (17 sts).

Row 16: ch 4, turn, sc in 2nd ch from hook and each remaining ch or st across (20 sts).

Rows 17-21: ch 1, turn, sc in each st across (20 sts).

Fasten off.

SLEEVES (MAKE 2)

With pink yarn, ch 16.

Rows 1-8: ch 1, turn, sc in each st across; change to gray yarn in last st of Row 8 (16 sts).

Row 9: ch 1, turn, sc in each st across (16 sts). Fasten off.

FINISHING

Sew front pieces to back at shoulders. Align center of sleeve with shoulder seam and sew in place (see Fig. A).

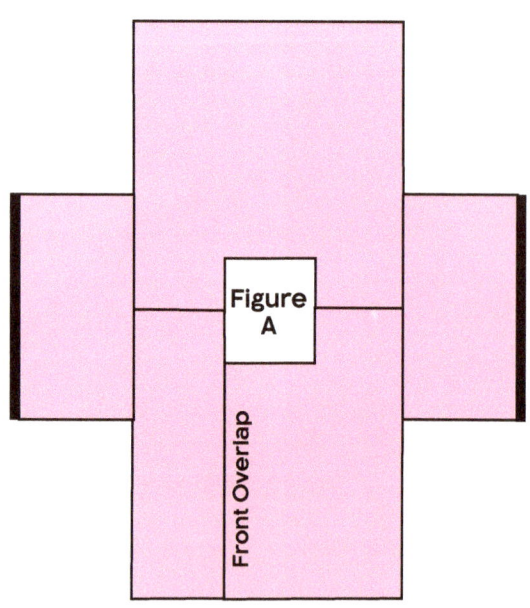

Figure A

Front Overlap

Fold piece in half crosswise so that hem edges of fronts and back meet (see Fig. B). Sew together along underarms and sides.

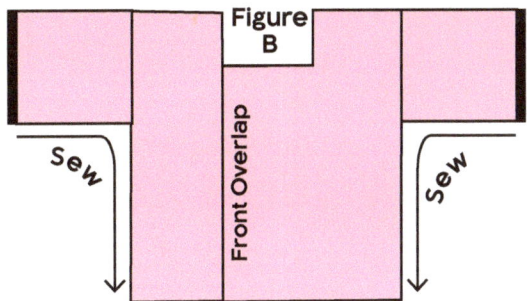

Smoothing the edge: Referring to Fig. C, join pink yarn with sc at black dot, sc in each st around hemline.

Fasten off.

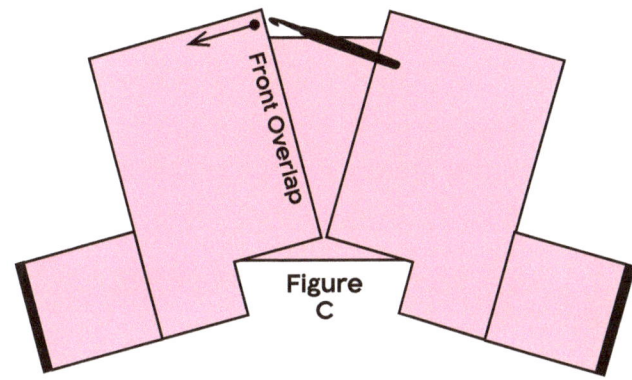

Smoothing the edge: Referring to Fig. D, join pink yarn with sc at black dot, sc in each st around neckline; change to gray yarn in last st (see turquoise dot).

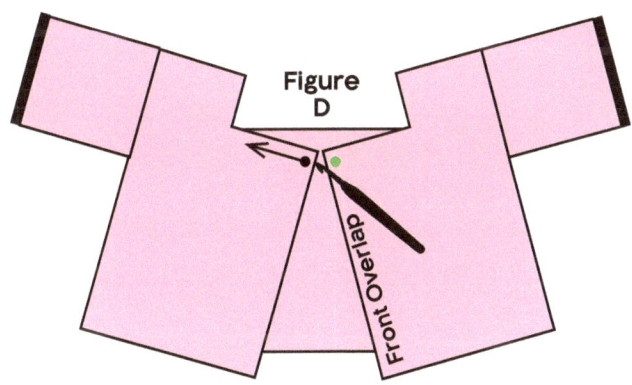

Gray Edgestitching: sc in each st along front edge, hemline, next front edge and neckline making 3 sts in same st at corners.

Fasten off. Weave in ends.

Sew buttons to front as shown in photo.

Sew ball side of 3 snap fasteners to wrong side of jacket front overlap. Sew socket side of snap fasteners to underlying jacket front to match up with ball side.

CHEF PANTS

The pants are crocheted in rounds, starting at the waist. Clear elastic bead cord makes great waistband elastic. It's super strong and very stretchy.

With multicolor yarn, ch 36, join with sl st in 1st ch to make a ring using care not to twist the chain.

Rnds 1-10: sc in each st around. Place marker for beginning of rnd and move marker up as each rnd is completed (36 sts).

Crotch: ch 2, skip 17 sts, sc in next st. This will divide ring in half for pant legs.

FIRST LEG

Rnd 11: sc in next 18 sts, sc in back loops of next 2 chs (20 sts).

Rnds 12-32: sc in each st around, try pants on doll as you near the final rnds and adjust length if needed (20 sts).

Sl st in next st. Fasten off.

SECOND LEG

Rnd 1: join with sc at remaining leg opening, sc in each st or ch around. Place marker for beginning of rnd and move marker up as each rnd is completed (20 sts).

Rnds 2-22: sc in each st around, try pants on doll as you near the final rnds and adjust length if needed (20 sts).

Sl st in next st. Fasten off.

FINISHING

Thread a yarn needle with elastic cord and weave through back of stitches around waist edge. Try pants on doll to get the right tension so it's not too loose or too tight. Tie a knot to secure elastic. Weave in ends.

CHEF HAT

The Chef Hat is crocheted from the top down.

With pink yarn, make a magic ring, ch 1.

Rnd 1: 6 sc in ring, pull ring closed tight (6 sts).

Rnd 2: 2 sc in each st around. Place marker for beginning of rnd and move marker up as each rnd is completed (12 sts).

Rnd 3: *sc in next st, 2 sc in next st* 6 times (18 sts).

Rnd 4: *sc in next 2 sts, 2 sc in next st* 6 times (24 sts).

Rnd 5: sc in each st around.

Rnd 6: *sc in next st, 2 sc in next st* 12 times (36 sts).

Rnd 7: sc in each st around.

Rnd 8: *sc in next 2 sts, 2 sc in next st* 12 times (48 sts).

Rnd 9: sc in each st around.

Rnd 10: *sc in next 3 sts, 2 sc in next st* 12 times (60 sts).

Rnd 11: sc in each st around.

Rnd 12: *sc in next 4 sts, 2 sc in next st* 12 times (72 sts).

Rnd 13: sc in each st around.

Rnd 14: *sc in next 5 sts, 2 sc in next st* 12 times (84 sts).

Rnd 15: sc in each st around.

Rnd 16: *sc in next 6 sts, 2 sc in next st* 12 times (96 sts).

Rnd 17: sc in each st around.

Rnd 18: *sc in next 7 sts, 2 sc in next st* 12 times (108 sts).

Rnd 19: sc in each st around.

Rnd 20: *sc in next 8 sts, 2 sc in next st* 12 times (120 sts).

Rnd 21: sc in each st around.

Rnd 22: *sc in next 9 sts, 2 sc in next st* 12 times (132 sts).

Rnd 23: sc in each st around.

Rnd 24: *sc in next 10 sts, 2 sc in next st* 12 times (144 sts).

Rnd 25: sc in each st around.

Rnd 26: *sc in next 11 sts, 2 sc in next st* 12 times (156 sts).

Rnd 27: sc in each st around.

Rnd 28: *sc in next 12 sts, 2 sc in next st* 12 times (168 sts).

Rnd 29: sc in each st around.

Rnd 30: *sc in next 12 sts, 2 sc in next st* 12 times (180 sts).

Rnd 31: sc3tog around (60 sts).

Rnds 32-38: sc in each st around.

Sl st in next st. Fasten off. Weave in ends.

BOW

All sts of the Bow, except the chs, are worked into a ring.

With gray yarn, ch 4, join with sl st in 1st ch to make a ring.

Rnd 1:

for **first loop**, ch 8, sl st in ring;

for **2nd loop**, make same as first loop;

for **first tail**, ch 6, turn, starting in 2nd ch from hook, sl st in next 5 chs, sl st in ring;

for **2nd tail**, make same as first tail;

to **finish loops**, 10 sc over one loop, sl st in ring; 10 sc over 2nd loop, sl st in ring. Fasten off.

To **finish bow**, wrap 1 tail tightly around center of bow 3 times, wrapping between loops and tails. Place bow wrong-side up and knot tails together. Sew to hat.

Half Apron

Oven Mitts

SUPPLIES

G6/4mm crochet hook

Small amount of Dark, Light Worsted yarn in dark blue and light blue

With dark blue yarn, make a magic ring, ch 1.

Rnd 1: 6 sc in ring, pull ring closed tight (6 sts).

Rnd 2: 2 sc in each st around. Place marker for beginning of rnd and move marker up as each rnd is completed (12 sts).

Rnd 3: *sc in next st, 2 sc in next st* 6 times (18 sts).

Rnds 4-6: sc in each st around.

Rnd 7: *sc in next st, sc2tog* 6 times (12 sts).

Rnds 8-9: sc in each st around; change to light blue yarn in last st of Rnd 9.

Tip: When working the next rnd, carry yarn tails from color change across top of previous rnd and crochet over them to encase the tails. This will result in fewer ends to weave in when done.

Rnd 10: sc in each st around.

Sl st in next st. Fasten off. Weave in ends.

SUPPLIES

G6/4mm crochet hook

Small amount of DK, Light Worsted yarn in purple and pink

Note: A chain 1 at the beginning of a row is for turning your work and does not count as a stitch.

With purple yarn, loosely ch 14.

Row 1: ch 1, turn, 2 dc in each st across (28 sts).

Row 2: ch 1, turn, *dc in next st, 2 dc in each st* across (42 sts).

Rows 3-6: ch 1, turn, dc in each st across. Fasten off.

Next you will make the waist ties and waistband.

Row 7: for **1st tie**, ch 45; to connect at waistline, sc in top 14 chs of skirt; for **2nd tie**, ch 45 (14 sts, 90 chs).

Row 8: ch 1, turn, sc in each ch and st across (104 sts).

Fasten off. Weave in ends.

FINISHING

With a double strand of pink yarn, embroider thru the dc spaces of Row 5 with running stitch.

Full Apron

SUPPLIES

G6/4mm crochet hook

Small amount of DK, Light Worsted yarn in gray and pink

Glue (for fabric, see page 11)

Note: A chain 1 at the beginning of a row is for turning your work and does not count as a stitch.

SKIRT

With gray yarn, loosely ch 18.

Row 1: ch 1, turn, 2 dc in each ch across (36 sts).

Rows 2-6: ch 1, turn, dc in each st across.

Fasten off.

Next you will make the waist ties and waistband.

Row 7: for **1st tie**, ch 50; to connect at waistline, sc in top 18 chs of skirt; **for 2nd tie**, ch 50 (18 sts, 100 chs).

Row 8: ch 1, turn, sc in each ch and st across (118 sts). Fasten off.

BIB

Mark the center 10 sts of waistband. This is where you will work the bib. Join gray yarn at first marker.

Row 1: sc in each st across (10 sts).

Rows 2-8: ch 1, turn, sc in each st across.

Do not fasten off. For first **neck tie**, ch 50.

Row 9: ch 1, turn, sc in each ch across.

Sl st in next st to join tie to top of bib. Fasten off.

Join gray yarn at next corner of bib and make a 2nd identical tie.

Weave in ends.

HEART APPLIQUE

All sts of the heart, except the chs, are worked into a magic ring. When you tighten the ring, the heart will take shape like magic!

This pattern includes treble crochet. If you would like to see a video of treble crochet stitches being made in a ring, go to the 'Amigurumi Tutorials' board on my Pinterest page (see page 89) or search "treble crochet in a ring" at youtube.com.

With pink yarn, make a magic ring, ch 3.

Rnd 1: 3 tr, 3 dc, tr, 3 dc, 3 tr, ch 3, sl st. Pull ring closed tight. Fasten off.

Knot tails together and trim ends to 1/2". Glue to bib.

Cupcake Blouse

Two identical pieces are crocheted flat in rows and sewn together to make this easy top. A cupcake applique embellishes the front.

SUPPLIES

C2/2.75mm and G6/4mm crochet hooks

Small amount of DK, Light Worsted yarn in blue, tan, pink and red

Glue (for fabric, see page 11)

Note: A chain 1 at the beginning of a row is for turning your work and does not count as a stitch.

BLOUSE (MAKE 2)

With G6/4mm crochet hook and blue yarn, ch 18.

Rows 1-4: ch 1, turn, dc in each st across (18 sts).

Rows 5-7: ch 1, turn, dc in next 15 sts (15 sts).

Row 8: ch 4, turn, dc in 2nd ch from hook and each remaining ch or st across (18 sts).

Rows 9-11: ch 1, turn, dc in each st across (18 sts). Fasten off.

CUPCAKE APPLIQUE

Cupcake Bottom:

With C2/2.75mm crochet hook and tan yarn, ch 7.

Row 1: starting in 2nd ch from hook, sc in each ch across (6 sts).

Rows 2-7: ch 1, turn, working in **back loops only**, sc in each st across (6 sts). Fasten off.

Frosting:

With C2/2.75mm crochet hook and pink yarn, ch 2.

Row 1: 3 sc in 2nd ch from hook (3 sts).

Row 2: ch 1, turn, 2 sc in next 3 sts (6 sts).

Row 3: ch 1, turn, *sc in next st, 2 sc in next st* 3 times (9 sts).

Row 4: ch 1, turn, *sc in next 2 sts, 2 sc in next st* 3 times (12 sts).

Row 5: ch 1, do not turn; working forward across straight side, 5 sc in first st, skip next st, sl st in next st; 5 sc in middle st, skip next st, sl st in next st; 5 sc in last st. Fasten off.

Sew yarn tail down thru "V" of next st to smooth the edge.

Cherry: With C2/2.75mm crochet hook and red yarn, make a magic ring, ch 1.

Rnd 1: 5 hdc in ring, pull ring closed tight, join with sl st in first st. Fasten off.

Push on center of Rnd 1 to pop cherry into shape.

FINISHING

Stack blouse pieces and sew together across shoulders.

Sew up sides leaving 1" open to create armholes. Weave in ends.

Glue cupcake to front of blouse.

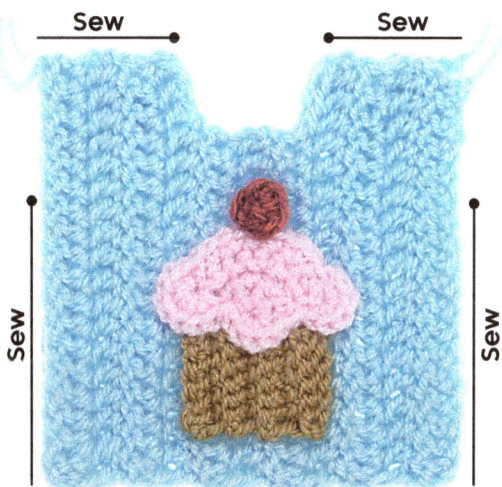

Pleated Skirt

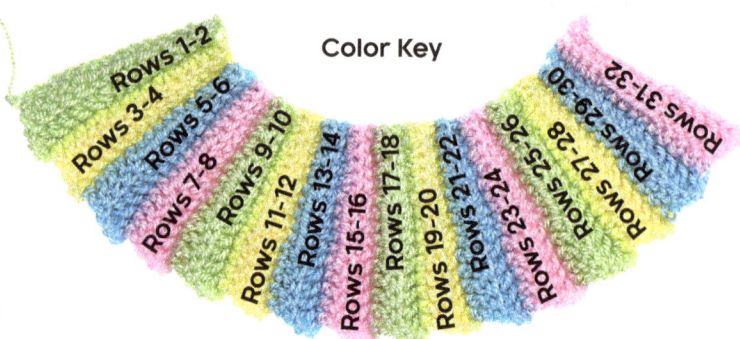

Color Key

The skirt is worked in rows, then connected with a seam at the back.

SUPPLIES

G6/4mm crochet hook

Small amount of DK, Light Worsted yarn in green, yellow, blue and pink

Stretch Magic clear elastic bead cord (.7mm)

Pattern Notes

• A chain 1 or chain 3 at the beginning of a row is for turning your work and does not count as a stitch. A ch 3 has only a decorative purpose, to create the wavy edge of the pleats.

• To change color, work last stitch of old color to last yarn over, yarn over with new color and pull thru both loops to complete the stitch. Pull gently on yarn strands to remove excess slack.

• After each color change, cut off unused yarn leaving a tail. Place tail over top of next stitch and complete stitch as normal so the tail is encased. Continue in this manner for the first 5 sc in your row, then trim the excess tail to 1/2". This securely hides tails in middle of stitches and eliminates the need to weave in a lot of ends.

SKIRT

How to Make Stripes: Each stripe consists of 2 rows. Refer to Color Key and change to next color in last st of every other row.

With green yarn, ch 15

Row 1: ch 1, turn, sc in first 5 ch, hdc in next 5 ch, dc in last 5 ch (15 sts).

Row 2: ch 3, turn, working in **back loops only**, dc in first 5 sts, hdc in next 5 sts, sc in last 5 sts; change to next color in last st (15 sts).

Row 3: ch 1, turn, working in **back loops only**, sc in first 5 sts, hdc in next 5 sts, dc in last 5 sts (15 sts).

Row 4: ch 3, turn, working in **back loops only**, dc in first 5 sts, hdc in next 5 sts, sc in last 5 sts; change to next color in last st (15 sts).

Rows 5-32: Repeat Rows 3-4.

Do not fasten off. Fold skirt with right sides facing so that first and last rows meet. Working thru **both loops**, sl st thru both layers stitch-for-stitch (15 sts).

Fasten off. Weave in end. Turn skirt right side out.

Back Side

FINISHING

Thread a blunt-tip yarn needle with elastic cord and weave thru stitches around top of skirt. Try skirt on doll to get the right tension and knot tails of elastic together. Weave in ends.

Boatneck Tunic

Rnd 2: ch 3 (counts as dc), 4 dc in same st, dc in next 2 sts, *5 dc in next st, dc in next 2 sts* 3 times, join with sl st in top of ch-3. Place marker for beginning of rnd and move marker up as each rnd is completed (27 sts, 3 chs.)

Tip: Place marker in middle of each 5-dc cluster and move marker up as next cluster is created.

Rnd 3: ch 3 (counts as dc), dc in next st, *5 dc in next st, dc in next 6 sts* 3 times, 5 dc in next st, dc in next 4 sts, join with sl st in top of ch-3 (43 sts, 3 chs).

Rnd 4: ch 3 (counts as dc), dc in next 4 sts, *5 dc in next st, dc in next 10 sts* 3 times, 5 dc in next st, dc in next 6 sts, join with sl st in top of ch-3 (60 sts, 3 chs).

Rnd 5: ch 3 (counts as dc), dc in next 6 sts, *5 dc in next st, dc in next 14 sts* 3 times, 5 dc in next st, dc in next 8 sts, join with sl st in top of ch-3 (76 sts, 3 chs). Fasten off.

To create **neckline**, place each square as shown below and fold 1" at Corner A to wrong side. Use ending tail to sew tip in place.

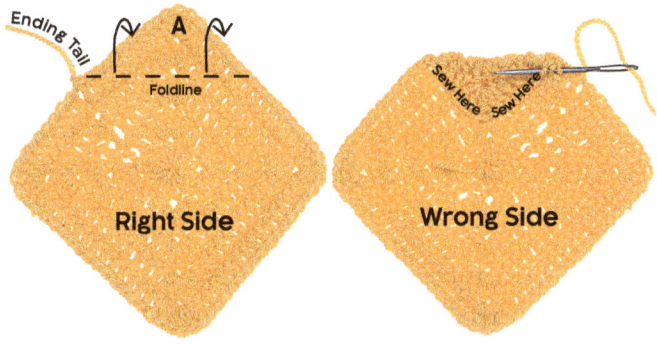

For **underarm seam**, stack squares with wrong sides facing and sew 5 stitches together as shown below.

Choose a thin brand of DK yarn for the tunic. This will minimize bulk at the neckline and provide nice drape for the tunic's flowy style.

The bodice pieces are made from dc squares worked in the round. The corners are started in Rnd 2 with clusters of 5 dc. In subsequent rnds, the corners are maintained with new 5-dc clusters in center st of previous corner.

SUPPLIES

G6/4mm crochet hook

Small amount of DK, Light Worsted yarn in yellow & purple

BODICE (MAKE 2)

Make a magic ring, ch 2 (does not count as dc).

Rnd 1: 12 dc in ring, pull ring closed tight, join with sl st in top of first dc (12 sts).

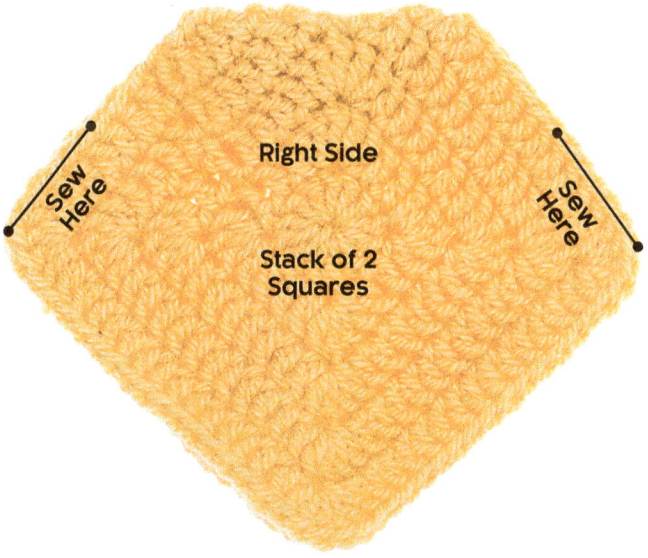

SLEEVES (MAKE 2)

Insert hook thru both layers at red dot **X** (see photo above), join new yarn and knot it to close up neckline securely, ch 1.

Rnd 1: 17 dc around armhole edge (17 sts).

Rnds 2-4: dc in each st around.

Sl st in next st. Fasten off. Weave in ends.

Insert hook thru both layers at red dot **Y** and repeat for 2nd sleeve.

BOW

The Bow has 2 flat 'loops' and 2 tails. All sts of the bow, except the chs, are worked into a magic ring. If you would like to see a video of treble crochet stitches being made in a ring, go to the 'Amigurumi Tutorials' board on my Pinterest page (see page 89) or search "treble crochet in a ring" at youtube.com.

Make a magic ring, ch 4.

Rnd 1:

for **first loop**, 3 tr in ring, ch 4, sl st in ring;

for **2nd loop**, ch 4, 3 tr in ring, ch 4, sl st in ring;

for **first tail**, ch 6, turn, starting in 2nd ch from hook, sc in next 5 chs, sl st in ring;

for **2nd tail**, make same as first tail.

Fasten off. Pull ring closed tight.

To finish, pull ending tail to back and wrap it tightly around center of bow 4 times, wrapping between loops and tails.

Place bow wrong-side up and knot tails together. Sew to front of tunic.

Tulip Pants

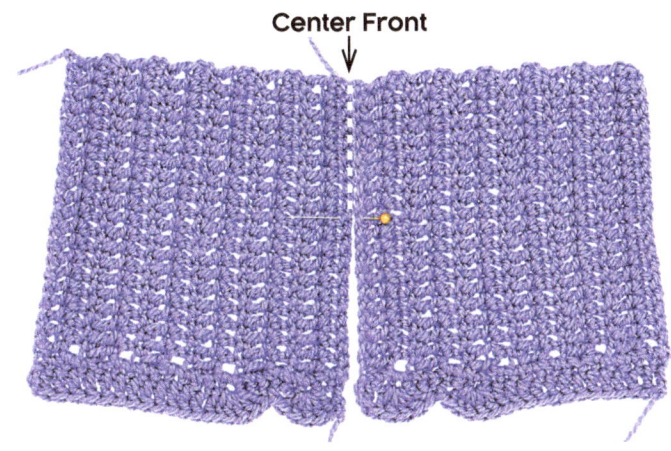

SIDE 2

Make the same as Side 1 through Row 13.

Row 14: for **tulip hem**, ch 1, turn, dc in next 13 sts, 5 dc in next st, skip next 2 sts, sl st in next st, skip next 2 sts, 5 dc in next st, skip next st, dc in next st.

Fasten off.

Place pieces side-by-side as shown in picture below. For **center front** seam, sew top 10 sts together. Repeat for **center back** seam. To form **legs**, sew first and last rows together on each side.

SUPPLIES

G6/4mm crochet hook

Small amount of DK, Light Worsted yarn

Stretch Magic clear elastic bead cord (.7mm)

Note: A chain 1 at the beginning of a row is for turning your work and does not count as a stitch.

SIDES (MAKE 2)

SIDE 1

Ch 20 loosely.

Rows 1-12: ch 1, turn, dc in each st across (20 sts).

Row 13: ch 1, do not turn, continue working forward and make 22 sc evenly spaced across next side (22 sts). This will be bottom of pants.

Row 14: for **tulip hem**, ch 1, turn, dc in next st, skip next st, 5 dc in next st, skip next 2 sts, sl st in next st, skip next 2 sts, 5 dc in next st, dc in next 13 sts.

Fasten off.

WAISTBAND

Join with sc at center back.

Rnd 1: sc in each st around. Fasten off. Weave in ends.

FINISHING

Thread a yarn needle with elastic cord and weave through back of stitches around waist edge. Try pants on doll to get the right tension so it's not too loose or too tight. Tie a knot to secure elastic and weave in ends.

Chocolate Chip Cookie Purse

Rnd 7: *sc in next 5 sts, 2 sc in next st* 6 times (42 sts).

Sl st in next st. Fasten off. Weave in ends.

FINISHING

For **chocolate chips**, embroider French Knots (see page 88) on 1 circle with brown yarn as pictured. For the best results, pierce yarn strands to make French Knots (do not work in the holes between stitches).

Place the 2 circles together with wrong sides facing. Set aside.

For **handle**, ch 45 with tan yarn; now **connect the circles** by working 28 sc thru sts around edge of both circles. Join to beginning of ch and continue sc across the ch.

Sl st in next st. Fasten off. Weave in ends.

SUPPLIES

G6/4mm crochet hook

Small amount of DK, Light Worsted yarn in tan and brown

CIRCLES (MAKE 2)

With tan yarn, make a magic ring, ch 1.

Rnd 1: 6 sc in ring, pull ring closed tight (6 sts).

Rnd 2: 2 sc in each st around. Place marker for beginning of rnd and move marker up as each rnd is completed (12 sts).

Rnd 3: *sc in next st, 2 sc in next st* 6 times (18 sts).

Rnd 4: sc in next st, 2 sc in next st, *sc in next 2 sts, 2 sc in next st* 5 times, sc in next st (24 sts).

Rnd 5: *sc in next 3 sts, 2 sc in next st* 6 times (30 sts).

Rnd 6: sc in next 2 sts, 2 sc in next st, *sc in next 4 sts, 2 sc in next st* 5 times, sc in next 2 sts (36 sts).

Confetti Donut Purse

Multi-colored stitches can be embroidered for the sprinkles as an alternative to bugle beads.

SUPPLIES

G6/4mm crochet hook

Small amount of DK, Light Worsted yarn in pink and white

Bugle beads in assorted colors, 6mm

Glue (for beads & fabric, see page 11)

CIRCLES (MAKE 2)

With pink yarn, make a magic ring, ch 1.

Rnd 1: 6 sc in ring, pull ring closed tight (6 sts).

Rnd 2: 2 sc in each st around. Place marker for beginning of rnd and move marker up as each rnd is completed (12 sts).

Rnd 3: *sc in next st, 2 sc in next st* 6 times (18 sts).

Rnd 4: sc in next st, 2 sc in next st, *sc in next 2 sts, 2 sc in next st* 5 times, sc in next st (24 sts).

Rnd 5: *sc in next 3 sts, 2 sc in next st* 6 times (30 sts).

Rnd 6: sc in next 2 sts, 2 sc in next st, *sc in next 4 sts, 2 sc in next st* 5 times, sc in next 2 sts (36 sts).

Rnd 7: *sc in next 5 sts, 2 sc in next st* 6 times (42 sts).

Sl st in next st. Fasten off. Weave in ends.

Place the 2 circles together with wrong sides facing. Set aside.

For **handle**, ch 45 with pink yarn; now **connect the circles** by working 28 sc thru sts around edge of both circles. Join to beginning of ch and continue sc across the ch.

Sl st in next st. Fasten off. Weave in ends.

FROSTING

With white yarn, ch 18, join with sl st in 1st ch to make a ring.

Rnd 1: sc in each ch around (18 sts).

Rnd 2: sc in next st, 2 sc in next st, *sc in next 2 sts, 2 sc in next st* 5 times, sc in next st (24 sts).

Rnd 3: *sc in next 3 sts, 2 sc in next st* 6 times (30 sts).

The next rnd alternates scallops and picots to create the wavy edge.

Rnd 4: *5 sc in next st, skip next st, sl st in next st; ch 3, sc in back bar of 3rd ch from hook, sl st in next st* around. Fasten off.

FINISHING

Glue frosting to one side of purse.

For **sprinkles**, glue bugle beads randomly to frosting.

Tea Party Purse

An easy 3-round doily creates the flap for the purse.

SUPPLIES

G6/4mm crochet hook

Small amount of DK, Light Worsted yarn in white & lavender

Sewing thread

1 button, 1/2" diameter

DOILY

A chain space refers to a hole left in your work by making chain stitches. When you are instructed to crochet into a chain space, just insert your hook into the space underneath the chain to make your stitch.

With white yarn, ch 4.

Rnd 1: 9 dc in 4th ch from hook, join with sl st in 1st dc to make a ring (9 sts).

Rnd 2: ch 4, sc in same st as where your ch started, *ch 3, sc in next st* 8 times; **ch 3**, join with sl st in next st (10 chain loops).

Round 2

Round 3

Rnd 3: sl st twice in next chain space, ch 5, sc in next chain space, *ch 4, sc in next chain space* 8 times; **ch 4**, join with sl st in starting sl st (10 chain loops).

Fasten off.

BAG

The bag is worked from the bottom up. It is worked around a foundation chain.

With lavender yarn, ch 11.

Rnd 1: 2 hdc in 2nd ch from hook, hdc in next 8 chs, 4 hdc in next ch, hdc in next 8 chs, 2 hdc in last ch. Place marker for beginning of rnd and move marker up as each rnd is completed (24 sts).

Rnd 2: working in **back loops only** (see page 86), sc in each st around (24 sts).

Rnds 3-8: resuming work in **both loops,** sc in each st around (24 sts).

Sl st in next 3 sts to reach handle location at side of bag (see pink dots below). Do not fasten off.

For **handle**, ch 20, sc in opposite side of bag where handle should connect (see pink dots below), turn, sl st in each ch across. Fasten off.

FINISHING

For **flap**, sew edge of doily to bag back as shown with dotted line above. Sew button to bag front. Weave in ends.

Tea Party Hat

The Tea Party Hat is worked from the top down in rounds. Worsted weight yarn gives it a sturdy structure. Ribbon can be substituted for the crocheted hat band if desired.

SUPPLIES

G6/4mm crochet hook

50 yds of Worsted weight yarn in blue

Small amount of Worsted weight yarn in white

HAT

With blue yarn, make a magic ring, ch 1.

Rnd 1: 6 sc in ring, pull ring closed tight (6 sts).

Rnd 2: 2 sc in each st around. Place marker for beginning of rnd and move marker up as each rnd is completed (12 sts).

Rnd 3: *sc in next st, 2 sc in next st* 6 times (18 sts).

Rnd 4: *sc in next 2 sts, 2 sc in next st* 6 times (24 sts).

Rnd 5: *sc in next 3 sts, 2 sc in next st* 6 times (30 sts).

Rnd 6: *sc in next 4 sts, 2 sc in next st* 6 times (36 sts).

Rnd 7: *sc in next 5 sts, 2 sc in next st* 6 times (42 sts).

Rnd 8: *sc in next 6 sts, 2 sc in next st* 6 times (48 sts).

Rnds 9-13: sc in each st around.

Rnd 14: dc in each st around.

Rnd 15: sc in each st around.

Next the ruffled brim is made.

Rnd 16: *sc in next st, 2 sc in next st* around (72 sts).

Rnd 17: *sc in next 2 sts, 2 sc in next st* around (96 sts).

Rnd 18: *sc in next 3 sts, 2 sc in next st* around (120 sts).

Sl st in next st. Fasten off. Weave in ends.

Shape brim into waves as shown in picture.

HAT BAND

With white yarn, chain a string 24" long. Thread tail into yarn needle and weave chain thru the dc spaces of Rnd 14 going *<u>under</u> post of next st, <u>over</u> posts of next 2 sts* around. Tie ends in a bow. Trim tails to 1/2".

Stole

Row 4: ch 1, turn, dc in first 31 sts, 3 dc in next st, dc in last 31 sts (65 sts).

Row 5: ch 1, turn, dc in first 32 sts, 3 dc in next st, dc in last 32 sts (67 sts).

Row 6: ch 1, turn, dc in first 33 sts, 3 dc in next st, dc in last 33 sts (69 sts).

Fasten off with 9" tail.

FINISHING

For **rounded end** of stole, thread yarn tail onto blunt-tipped yarn needle and weave tail thru sts across end. Push fabric along yarn tail and gather into desired shape. Knot tail, weave in end. Repeat at other end of stole.

You can brush the stole briskly with a stiff hair brush or a wire pet brush to create a fuzzy look if you wish. Use sparkly yarn for a touch of bling!

SUPPLIES

G6/4mm crochet hook

Small amount of DK, Light Worsted yarn

Note: A chain 1 at the beginning of a row is for turning your work and does not count as a stitch.

STOLE

Leaving a 9" starting tail, ch 57.

Row 1: ch 1, turn, dc in first 28 sts, 3 dc in next st, dc in last 28 sts (59 sts).

Row 2: ch 1, turn, dc in first 29 sts, 3 dc in next st, dc in last 29 sts (61 sts).

Row 3: ch 1, turn, dc in first 30 sts, 3 dc in next st, dc in last 30 sts (63 sts).

Lace Nightgown

The nightgown is made from the top down using rows for the yoke, then joined to work the skirt in rounds. Make a shorter version for a cute sundress (see photo page 30).

The lace is created from stitch patterns that resemble little shells. To make a shell, multiple stitches are worked into the same stitch.

A chain space refers to a hole left in your work by making chain stitches. When you are instructed to crochet into a chain space, just insert your hook into the space underneath the chain to make your stitch.

SUPPLIES

G6/4mm crochet hook

Small amount of DK, Light Worsted yarn

1 button, 1/2" diameter

2 buttons, 1/4" diameter

Sewing thread

Note: A chain 1 at the beginning of a row is for turning your work and does not count as a stitch.

★ SPECIAL STITCH USED IN THIS PATTERN
SHELL STITCH (2 dc, ch 1, 2 dc, ch 1)

NIGHTGOWN

With a 12" starting tail, ch 24.

Row 1: ch 1, turn, sc in each ch across (24 sts).

Row 2: ch 1, turn, sc in next 4 sts; for **armhole**, ch 7 loosely, skip next 3 sts; sc in next 10 sts; for **armhole**, ch 7 loosely, skip next 3 sts; sc in next 4 sts (18 sts, 14 chs).

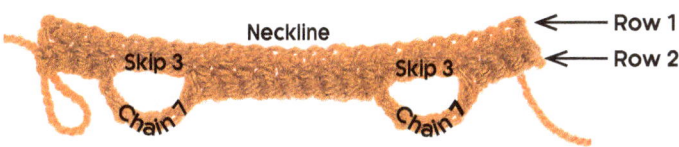

Rows 3-6: ch 1, turn, sc in each st or ch across (32 sts).

Join Row 6 with sl st in first st. Now work in continuous rnds.

Rnd 7: *shell in next st, skip next st* 16 times. Place marker for beginning of rnd and move marker up as each rnd is completed (16 shells).

Rnds 8-19: shell in ch-1 space of each shell around (16 shells). See photo below.

Black Dots = Ch-1 Spaces of Shells

Sl st in ch-1 space of next shell. Fasten off.

FINISHING

For **button loop**, insert hook in 1st st of Row 1 and pull up a loop of yarn from starting tail, ch 5, sl st in next st. Fasten off. Weave in ends. Sew 1/2" button to corner opposite button loop. Sew 1/4" buttons to center front.

35

Mary Janes

SUPPLIES

G6/4mm crochet hook

Small amount of DK Light Worsted yarn

2 buttons, 1/2" diameter

Sewing Thread

RIGHT SHOE

Ch 6. Next you will crochet around the chain.

Rnd 1: for **sole**, starting in 2nd ch from hook, sc in next 4 chs, 3 sc in next ch, sc in next 3 chs, 2 sc in last ch. Place marker for beginning of rnd and move marker up as each rnd is completed (12 sts).

Rnd 2: 2 sc in next st, sc in next 3 sts, 2 sc in next 3 sts, sc in next 3 sts, 2 sc in next 2 sts (18 sts).

Rnd 3: 2 sc in next st, sc in next 4 sts, 2 sc in next st, *sc in next st, 2 sc in next st* twice, sc in next 4 sts, *2 sc in next st, sc in next st* twice (24 sts).

Rnd 4: working in **back loops only**, sc in each st around.

Rnds 5-6: resuming work in **both loops**, sc in each st around.

Rnd 7: sc in next 8 sts, sc2tog 4 times, sc in next 8 sts (20 sts).

Rnd 8: sl st in next 5 sts; for **strap**, ch 20, sl st in same stitch as where your chain started; sl st in each remaining st around (21 sts, 20 chs). Fasten off. Weave in ends.

Sew button opposite strap (10 sts between button & strap).

LEFT SHOE

Rnds 1-7: follow instructions for right shoe.

Rnd 8: sl st in next 15 sts, for **strap**, ch 20, sl st in same stitch as where your chain started, sl st in each remaining st around (21 sts, 20 chs). Fasten off. Weave in ends.

Sew button opposite strap (10 sts between button & strap).

Chef Shoes

SUPPLIES

G6/4mm crochet hook

Small amount of DK Light Worsted yarn in black and gray

With gray yarn, ch 6. Next you will crochet around the chain.

Rnd 1: for **sole**, starting in 2nd ch from hook, sc in next 4 chs, 3 sc in next ch, sc in next 3 chs, 2 sc in last ch. Place marker for beginning of rnd and move marker up as each rnd is completed (12 sts).

Rnd 2: 2 sc in next st, sc in next 3 sts, 2 sc in next 3 sts, sc in next 3 sts, 2 sc in next 2 sts (18 sts).

Rnd 3: 2 sc in next st, sc in next 4 sts, 2 sc in next st, *sc in next st, 2 sc in next st* twice, sc in next 4 sts, *2 sc in next st, sc in next st* twice (24 sts).

Rnd 4: working in **back loops only**, sc in each st around; change to black yarn in last st.

Rnds 5-7: resuming work in **both loops**, sc in each st around.

Rnd 8: sc in next 8 sts, sc2tog 4 times, sc in next 8 sts (20 sts).

Rnd 9: sl st in each st around. Fasten off.

Make a second identical shoe.

Sprinkle Slippers

Make sweet little donuts for Charlotte's feet!

SUPPLIES

G6/4mm crochet hook

Small amount of DK Light Worsted yarn in tan and pink

Bugle beads in assorted colors, 6mm

Glue (for beads, see page 11)

With tan yarn, ch 6. Next you will crochet around the chain.

Rnd 1: for **sole**, starting in 2nd ch from hook, sc in next 4 chs, 3 sc in next ch, sc in next 3 chs, 2 sc in last ch. Place marker for beginning of rnd and move marker up as each rnd is completed (12 sts).

Rnd 2: 2 sc in next st, sc in next 3 sts, 2 sc in next 3 sts, sc in next 3 sts, 2 sc in next 2 sts (18 sts).

Rnd 3: 2 sc in next st, sc in next 4 sts, 2 sc in next st, *sc in next st, 2 sc in next st* twice, sc in next 4 sts, *2 sc in next st, sc in next st* twice (24 sts).

Rnd 4: working in **back loops only**, sc in each st around.

Rnd 5: resuming work in **both loops**, sc in each st around; change to pink yarn in last st.

Rnd 6: sc in each st around.

Rnd 7: working in **back loops only**, sc in each st around.

Rnd 8: resuming work in **both loops**, sc in next 8 sts, sc2tog 4 times, sc in next 8 sts (20 sts).

Rnd 9: sc in next 7 sts, sc2tog 3 times, sc in next 7 sts (17 sts).

Sl st in next st. Fasten off.

Thread a blunt-tipped yarn needle with a double strand of pink yarn. Embroider up and down thru unworked front loops of Rnd 4 to make a wavy line.

Weave in ends.

Glue bugle beads to pink area.

Make a second identical slipper.

Booties

The booties have 2-layer soles. The bottom layer is worked separately in a contrasting color and attached with slip stitch.

SUPPLIES

G6/4mm crochet hook

Small amount of DK Light Worsted yarn in green & yellow

With green yarn, ch 6. Next you will crochet around the chain.

Rnd 1: for **1st sole**, starting in 2nd ch from hook, sc in next 4 chs, 3 sc in next ch, sc in next 3 chs, 2 sc in last ch. Place marker for beginning of rnd and move marker up as each rnd is completed (12 sts).

Rnd 2: 2 sc in next st, sc in next 3 sts, 2 sc in next 3 sts, sc in next 3 sts, 2 sc in next 2 sts (18 sts).

Rnd 3: 2 sc in next st, sc in next 4 sts, 2 sc in next st, *sc in next st, 2 sc in next st* twice, sc in next 4 sts, *2 sc in next st, sc in next st* twice (24 sts).

Rnd 4: working in **back loops only**, sc in each st around.

Rnds 5-7: resuming work in **both loops**, sc in each st around.

Rnd 8: sc in next 8 sts, sc2tog 4 times, sc in next 8 sts (20 sts).

Rnd 9: sc in next 8 sts, sc2tog twice, sc in next 8 sts (18 sts).

Rnds 10-14: sc in each st around; change to yellow yarn in last st of Rnd 14.

For **edge trim**, *sl st in next st, ch 3, sl st in same stitch as where your chain started, skip next st* around. Sl st in next st. Fasten off.

For **2nd sole**, use yellow yarn and repeat Rnds 1-3. Do not fasten off. Place wrong side against bottom of bootie with sts aligned. Sl st soles together working thru both loops of 2nd sole and unworked front loops of 1st sole. Fasten off. Weave in ends.

Make a second identical bootie.

37

Tablecloth

The tablecloth is worked in rounds with dc. A chain space refers to a hole left in your work by making chain stitches. You will see them abbreviated as "ch-1 space" and "ch-2 space". When you are instructed to crochet into a chain space, just insert your hook into the space underneath the chain to make your stitches.

Be sure to include the starting ch-3 as a dc when you confirm your stitch count for a round.

SUPPLIES

H8/5mm crochet hook

250 yds of Worsted weight yarn

SIZE 19" diameter

Ch 6, join with sl st in 1st ch to form a ring.

Rnd 1: ch 3 (*counts as dc*); **ch 1**, *dc, ch 1* 11 times in ring, join with sl st in top of ch-3. A half-inch diameter hole should remain in the middle (12 open spaces).

Rnd 2: ch 3 (*counts as dc*); 2 dc in next ch-1 space, *dc in front loop of next st, 2 dc in next ch-1 space* 11 times, join with sl st in top of ch-3. Place marker for beginning of rnd and move marker up as each rnd is completed (36 sts).

Rnd 3: ch 3 (*counts as dc*); **ch 2**, *skip 1 st, dc in next st, ch 2* 17 times, join with sl st in top of ch-3 (18 open spaces).

Rnd 4: ch 3 (*counts as dc*); 3 dc in next ch-2 space, *dc in next st, 3 dc in next ch-2 space* 17 times, join with sl st in top of ch-3 (72 sts).

Rnd 5: ch 3 (*counts as dc*); **ch 2**, *skip 1 st, dc in next st, ch 2* 35 times, join with sl st in top of ch-3 (36 open spaces).

Rnd 6: ch 3 (*counts as dc*); 2 dc in next ch-2 space, *dc in next st, 2 dc in next ch-2 space* 35 times, join with sl st in top of ch-3 (108 sts).

Rnds 7-9: ch 3 (*counts as dc*); dc in each st around, join with sl st in top of ch-3 (108 sts).

Rnd 10: ch 3 (*counts as dc*); dc in next 7 sts, 2 dc in next st, *dc in next 8 sts, 2 dc in next st* 11 times, join with sl st in top of ch-3 (120 sts).

Rnd 11: ch 3 (*counts as dc*); dc in next 8 sts, 2 dc in next st, *dc in next 9 sts, 2 dc in next st* 11 times, join with sl st in top of ch-3 (132 sts).

Rnd 12: ch 3 (*counts as dc*); dc in next 9 sts, 2 dc in next st, *dc in next 10 sts, 2 dc in next st* 11 times, join with sl st in top of ch-3 (144 sts).

Rnd 13: ch 3 (*counts as dc*); dc in next 10 sts, 2 dc in next st, *dc in next 11 sts, 2 dc in next st* 11 times, join with sl st in top of ch-3 (156 sts).

Rnd 14: ch 3 (*counts as dc*); dc in next 11 sts, 2 dc in next st, *dc in next 12 sts, 2 dc in next st* 11 times, join with sl st in top of ch-3 (168 sts).

Rnd 15: ch 3 (*counts as dc*); dc in next 12 sts, 2 dc in next st, *dc in next 13 sts, 2 dc in next st* 11 times, join with sl st in top of ch-3 (180 sts).

Rnd 16: ch 3 (*counts as dc*); dc in next 13 sts, 2 dc in next st, *dc in next 14 sts, 2 dc in next st* 11 times, join with sl st in top of ch-3 (192 sts).

Rnd 17: ch 3 (*counts as dc*); dc in next 14 sts, 2 dc in next st, *dc in next 15 sts, 2 dc in next st* 11 times, join with sl st in top of ch-3 (204 sts).

Rnd 18: for **scallops**, *skip next 2 sts; (tr, ch 1) 4 times in next st, tr in same st; skip next 2 sts; sl st in next st* 34 times (34 scallops).

Fasten off. Weave in ends.

Scallop

Tea Pot

The body of the tea pot is worked in the round from the bottom up. The lid is removable with space inside for a tea bag.

SUPPLIES

G6/4mm crochet hook

Small amount of Worsted weight yarn in blue, pink & rust

Glue (for fabric, see page 11)

Polyester fiberfill stuffing

BODY

With blue yarn, make a magic ring, ch 1.

Rnd 1: 6 sc in ring, pull ring closed tight (6 sts).

Rnd 2: 2 sc in each st around. Place marker for beginning of rnd and move marker up as each rnd is completed (12 sts).

Rnd 3: *sc in next st, 2 sc in next st* 6 times (18 sts).

Rnd 4: *sc in next 2 sts, 2 sc in next st* 6 times (24 sts).

Rnd 5: working in **back loops only,** *sc in next 3 sts, 2 sc in next st* 6 times (30 sts).

Rnd 6: resuming work in **both loops**, *sc in next 4 sts, 2 sc in next st* 6 times (36 sts).

Rnd 7: sc in each st around.

Rnd 8: *sc in next 5 sts, 2 sc in next st* 6 times (42 sts).

Rnds 9-13: sc in each st around.

Rnd 14: *sc in next 5 sts, sc2tog* 6 times (36 sts).

Rnd 15: *sc in next 4 sts, sc2tog* 6 times (30 sts).

Rnd 16: *sc in next 3 sts, sc2tog* 6 times (24 sts).

Rnd 17: working in **front loops only,** sc in each st around.

Rnd 18: resuming work in **both loops**, sc in each st around. Sl st in next st. Fasten off.

TEA

With rust yarn, make a magic ring, ch 1.

Rnd 1: 6 sc in ring, pull ring closed tight (6 sts).

Rnd 2: 2 sc in each st around. Place marker for beginning of rnd and move marker up as each rnd is completed (12 sts).

Rnd 3: *sc in next st, 2 sc in next st* 6 times (18 sts).

Rnd 4: *sc in next 2 sts, 2 sc in next st* 6 times (24 sts).

Sl st in next st. Fasten off with extra long tail.

Stuff body half way. Place tea right-side up at open end of body and use tail to sew in place: sew stitch-for-stitch thru <u>unworked back loops</u> of Rnd 17 of body and <u>back bumps</u> of Rnd 4 of tea pausing to finish stuffing when a small gap remains. Hide tail inside.

Squeeze into shape.

BOTTOM RIM

Turn body upside down and join blue in any unworked front loop of Rnd 5.

Rnd 1: sc in each st around (24 sts).

Rnd 2: sl st in each st around. Fasten off.

Bottom Rim

HANDLE

With pink yarn, make a magic ring, ch 1.

Rnd 1: 5 sc in ring, pull ring closed tight (5 sts).

Rnds 2-25: sc in each st around. Fasten off.

SPOUT

With pink yarn, make a magic ring, ch 1.

Rnd 1: 4 sc in ring, pull ring closed tight (4 sts).

Rnd 2: 2 sc in each st around. Place marker for beginning of rnd and move marker up as each rnd is completed (8 sts).

Rnds 3-7: sc in each st around.

Rnd 8: sc in next 4 sts, 2 sc in next 4 sts (12 sts).

Rnds 9-10: sc in each st around.

Sl st in next st. Fasten off. Sew or glue spout to tea pot as shown in picture. Push Rnds 1-3 inside to create the spout's opening. Weave in ends.

LID

With pink yarn, make a magic ring, ch 1.

Rnd 1: 6 sc in ring, pull ring closed tight (6 sts).

Rnd 2: 2 sc in each st around. Place marker for beginning of rnd and move marker up as each rnd is completed (12 sts).

Rnd 3: *sc in next st, 2 sc in next st* 6 times (18 sts).

Rnd 4: *sc in next 2 sts, 2 sc in next st* 6 times (24 sts).

Rnd 5: *sc in next 3 sts, 2 sc in next st* 6 times (30 sts).

Rnds 6-8: sc in each st around.

Sl st in next st. Fasten off. Weave in end.

KNOB

With blue yarn, make a magic ring, ch 1.

Rnd 1: 5 sc in ring, pull ring closed tight (5 sts).

Rnd 2: 2 sc in each st around. Place marker for beginning of rnd and move marker up as each rnd is completed (10 sts).

Rnds 3-4: sc in each st around.

Sl st in next st. Fasten off. Stuff knob and sew to top of lid.

HEART APPLIQUE

With pink yarn, make a magic ring, ch 3. All sts except the chs are worked into the ring.

Rnd 1: 3 tr, 3 dc, tr, 3 dc, 3 tr, ch 3, sl st. Pull ring closed tight. Fasten off.

Knot tails together and trim ends to 1/2". Glue to front of tea pot.

Teaspoon

Get out your D hook to make the little eating utensils. The teaspoon is made in 1 piece starting with the handle.

SUPPLIES

D3/3.25mm crochet hook

Small amount of DK, Light Worsted yarn in gray

Make a magic ring, ch 1.

Rnd 1: 5 sc in ring, pull ring closed tight (5 sts).

Rnds 2-8: sc in each st around.

Rnd 9: for **bowl**, *2 sc in next st, sc in next 2 sts, 2 sc in next st, sc in next st (7 sts).

Rnd 10: 2 sc in next st, sc in next 2 sts, 2 sc in next st, sc in next 3 sts (9 sts).

Rnd 11: *2 sc in next st, sc in next 2 sts* 3 times (12 sts).

Rnds 12-14: sc in each st around.

Rnd 15: *sc in next st, skip next st* 6 times (6 sts).

Rnd 16: sc in each st around.

Fasten off with extra long tail. Thread tail onto needle, weave needle under sts around opening and pull tight to close hole. Sew remaining tail up and down thru length of spoon several times. This will stuff the handle. Finger-press bowl to flatten.

MORE UTENSILS

Place settings of silverware are also provided as paper cut-outs.

See page 95.

Fork

The fork is made in 1 piece starting with the handle. Glue is used to stiffen the tines. Your favorite brand of white glue will do fine.

SUPPLIES

D3/3.25mm crochet hook

Small amount of DK, Light Worsted yarn in gray

Clear-drying white craft glue

Brush

Make a magic ring, ch 1.

Rnd 1: 5 sc in ring, pull ring closed tight (5 sts).

Rnds 2-11: sc in each st around.

Rnd 12: 2 sc in next st, sc in next 2 sts, 2 sc in next st, sc in next st (7 sts).

Rnd 13: 2 sc in next st, sc in next 2 sts, 2 sc in next st, sc in next 3 sts (9 sts).

Rnd 14: *2 sc in next st, sc in next 2 sts* 3 times (12 sts).

Flatten Rnd 14.

Row 15: for 2 tines, *ch 5, starting in 2nd ch from hook, sl st in next 4 chs, working thru both layers, sl st in next 2 sts* twice; for **3rd tine**, ch 5, starting in 2nd ch from hook, sl st in next 4 chs, working thru both layers, sl st in last st.

Fasten off with extra long tail. Sew tail up and down thru length of handle several times. This will stuff the handle.

FINISHING

To stiffen: In a small dish, stir together a mixture of approximately 60% glue and 40% water. The mixture is very forgiving, so don't worry about measuring. Brush glue mixture on back side of tines. Push tines into shape. Let dry.

Knife

The knife is made in 1 piece starting with the handle. Glue is used to stiffen the blade. Your favorite brand of white glue will do fine.

SUPPLIES

D3/3.25mm crochet hook

Small amount of DK, Light Worsted yarn in gray

Clear-drying white craft glue

Brush

Make a magic ring, ch 1.

Rnd 1: 5 sc in ring, pull ring closed tight (5 sts).

Rnds 2-11: sc in each st around.

Rnd 12: for **blade**, ch 10, starting in 2nd ch from hook, sc in next ch, hdc in next ch, dc in next ch, tr in next 3 chs, dc in next ch, hdc in next ch, sc in last ch (9 sts).

Fasten off with extra long tail. Sew blade to handle.

Sew tail up and down thru length of handle several times. This will stuff the handle.

FINISHING

To stiffen: In a small dish, stir together a mixture of approximately 60% glue and 40% water. The mixture is very forgiving, so don't worry about measuring. Brush glue mixture on back side of blade. Push blade into shape. Let dry.

Cream Pitcher

A circle of cream is sewn to the top of the pitcher before it is stuffed. A bottom rim allows the vessel to sit on the tablecloth without toppling over.

SUPPLIES

G6/4mm crochet hook

Small amount of Worsted weight yarn in pink, blue & white

Polyester fiberfill stuffing

PITCHER

With pink yarn, make a magic ring, ch 1.

Rnd 1: 8 sc in ring, pull ring closed tight (8 sts).

Rnd 2: 2 sc in each st around. Place marker for beginning of rnd and move marker up as each rnd is completed (16 sts).

Rnd 3: *sc in next st, 2 sc in next st* 8 times (24 sts).

Rnd 4: working in **back loops only**, sc in each st around.

Rnd 5: resuming work in **both loops**, sc in each st around.

Rnd 6: *sc in next st, sc2tog* 8 times (16 sts).

Rnd 7: sc in each st around.

Rnd 8: working in **front loops only**, *sc in next st, 2 sc in next st* 8 times (24 sts).

In the next round, the spout is made.

Rnd 9: resuming work in **both loops**, sc in next 9 sts, hdc in next st, dc in next st, 2 dc in next 2 sts, dc in next st, hdc in next st, sc in next 9 sts (26 sts).

Sl st in next st; change to blue yarn in the sl st.

For **handle,** loosely ch 12.

Row 10: working under **back bumps** of chs, sl st in 2nd ch from hook and in each remaining ch across.

Sl st in next st to join handle to top of pitcher. Fasten off.

Mark desired location for bottom end of handle.

BOTTOM RIM

Turn pitcher upside down, join pink yarn in unworked front loop of Rnd 4 at marked location for bottom end of handle.

Rnd 1: sc in each st around (24 sts).

Rnd 2: sl st in each st around. Fasten off.

Use tail to sew bottom of handle in place.

CREAM

With white yarn, make a magic ring, ch 1.

Rnd 1: 8 sc in ring, pull ring closed tight (8 sts).

Rnd 2: 2 sc in each st around (16 sts).

Sl st in next st. Fasten off with extra long tail.

Place cream right-side up at top of pitcher and use tail to sew in place: sew stitch-for-stitch thru unworked back loops of Rnd 9 of pitcher and back bumps of Rnd 2 of cream pausing to stuff when a small gap remains. Hide tail inside.

Squeeze pitcher into shape.

Sugar Bowl

A bottom rim allows the sugar bowl to sit nicely on the table cloth. A circle of sugar is sewn to the top of the bowl before it is stuffed.

SUPPLIES

G6/4mm crochet hook

Small amount of Worsted weight yarn in pink, blue & white

Polyester fiberfill stuffing

BOWL

With pink yarn, make a magic ring, ch 1.

Rnd 1: 8 sc in ring, pull ring closed tight (8 sts).

Rnd 2: 2 sc in each st around. Place marker for beginning of rnd and move marker up as each rnd is completed (16 sts).

Rnd 3: *sc in next st, 2 sc in next st* 8 times (24 sts).

Rnd 4: working in **back loops only,** sc in each st around.

Rnd 5: resuming work in **both loops,** sc in each st around.

Rnd 6: *sc in next st, sc2tog* 8 times (16 sts).

Rnd 7: sc in each st around.

Rnd 8: working in **front loops only,** *sc in next st, 2 sc in next st* 8 times (24 sts).

Rnd 9: resuming work in **both loops,** sc in each st around. Sl st in next st. Fasten off.

BOTTOM RIM

Turn sugar bowl upside down and join pink yarn in an unworked front loop of Rnd 4.

Rnd 1: sc in each st around (24 sts).

Rnd 2: sl st in each st around. Fasten off.

SUGAR

With white yarn, make a magic ring, ch 1.

Rnd 1: 8 sc in ring, pull ring closed tight (8 sts).

Rnd 2: 2 sc in each st around (16 sts).

Sl st in next st. Fasten off with extra long tail.

Place sugar right-side up at top of bowl and use tail to sew in place: sew stitch-for-stitch thru unworked back loops of Rnd 9 of bowl and back bumps of Rnd 2 of sugar pausing to stuff when a small gap remains. Hide tail inside.

Squeeze sugar bowl into shape.

LID

With blue yarn, make a magic ring, ch 1.

Rnd 1: 8 sc in ring, pull ring closed tight (8 sts).

Rnd 2: 2 sc in each st around (16 sts).

Rnd 3: *sc in next 7 sts, 2 sc in next st* 2 times (18 sts).

Rnd 4: sl st in each st around.

Fasten off. Weave in ends.

KNOB

With pink yarn, make a magic ring, ch 1.

Rnd 1: 4 sc in ring, pull ring closed tight (4 sts).

Rnd 2: *sc in next st, 2 sc in next st* twice (6 sts).

Rnd 3: sc in each st around.

Fasten off. Stuff knob and sew to top of lid.

Tea Cup & Saucer

The handle of the cup is made by working into the back bumps of a chain. This creates a lovely cord. Be sure to chain loosely or it will be difficult to push your hook into the bumps. When you turn your chain over, you will see the row of bumps.

SUPPLIES

G6/4mm crochet hook

Small amount of Worsted weight yarn in blue, pink & rust

Small amount of DK, Light Worsted yarn in pink (heart)

Glue (for fabric, see page 11)

Polyester fiberfill stuffing

CUP

With blue yarn, make a magic ring, ch 1.

Rnd 1: 6 sc in ring, pull ring closed tight (6 sts).

Rnd 2: 2 sc in each st around. Place marker for beginning of rnd and move marker up as each rnd is completed (12 sts).

Rnd 3: *sc in next st, 2 sc in next st* 6 times (18 sts).

Rnd 4: working in **back loops only**, sc in each st around.

Rnds 5-8: resuming work in **both loops**, sc in each st around.

Rnd 9: working in **front loops only**, sc in each st around.

Do not fasten off. **For handle**, loosely ch 12.

Row 10: working under **back bumps** of chs, sl st in 2nd ch from hook and in each remaining ch across.

Sl st in next st to join at top edge of cup. Fasten off. Mark desired location for bottom end of handle.

BOTTOM RIM

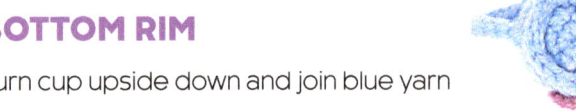

Turn cup upside down and join blue yarn in unworked front loop of Rnd 4 at marked location for bottom end of handle.

Rnd 1: sc in each st around (18 sts).

Rnd 2: sl st in each st around. Fasten off.

Use tail to sew bottom of handle in place.

TEA

With rust yarn, make a magic ring, ch 1.

Rnd 1: 6 sc in ring, pull ring closed tight (6 sts).

Rnd 2: 2 sc in each st around. Place marker for beginning of rnd and move marker up as each rnd is completed (12 sts).

Rnd 3: *sc in next st, 2 sc in next st* 6 times (18 sts).

Sl st in next st. Fasten off with extra long tail.

Place tea right-side up at top of cup and use tail to sew in place: sew stitch-for-stitch thru <u>unworked back loops</u> of Rnd 9 of cup and <u>back bumps</u> of Rnd 3 of tea pausing to stuff when a small gap remains. Hide tail inside.

Squeeze cup into shape.

HEART APPLIQUE

All sts except the chs are worked into a magic ring. When you close the ring, the heart will take shape like magic!

With DK Light Worsted yarn in pink, make a magic ring, ch 2.

Rnd 1: 2 dc, 2 hdc, dc, 2 hdc, 2 dc, ch 2, sl st. Pull ring closed tight. Fasten off.

Knot tails together, trim ends to 1/2". Glue to front of cup.

SAUCER

With Worsted Weight yarn in pink, make a magic ring, ch 1.

Rnd 1: 6 sc in ring, pull ring closed tight (6 sts).

Rnd 2: 2 sc in each st around. Place marker for beginning of rnd and move marker up as each rnd is completed (12 sts).

Rnd 3: *sc in next st, 2 sc in next st* 6 times (18 sts).

Rnd 4: sc in next st, 2 sc in next st, *sc in next 2 sts, 2 sc in next st* 5 times, sc in next st (24 sts).

Rnd 5: *sc in next 3 sts, 2 sc in next st* 6 times (30 sts).

Rnd 6: *sc in next 5 sts, 2 sc in next st* 5 times (35 sts).

Rnd 7: sl st in each st around. Fasten off. Weave in ends.

Tea Napkin

The Tea Napkin is crocheted in continuous rounds. Tiny scallops on the edge make it fancy!

SUPPLIES

F5/3.75mm crochet hook

Small amount of DK, Light Worsted yarn in white and pink

With white yarn,, make a magic ring, ch 1.

Rnd 1: 4 sc in ring, pull ring closed tight (4 sts).

Rnd 2: 3 sc in each st around. Place marker for beginning of rnd and move marker up as each rnd is completed (12 sts).

Rnd 3: sc in next st, 3 sc in next st, *sc in next 2 sts, 3 sc in next st* 3 times, sc in next st (20 sts).

Rnd 4: sc in next 2 sts, 3 sc in next st, *sc in next 4 sts, 3 sc in next st* 3 times, sc in next 2 sts (28 sts).

Rnd 5: sc in next 3 sts, 3 sc in next st, *sc in next 6 sts, 3 sc in next st* 3 times, sc in next 3 sts; change to pink yarn in last st (36 sts).

Rnd 6: for **scalloped edge**, *3 sc in next st, skip 1 st, sl st in next st* around. Fasten off. Weave in ends.

Napkin Ring

SUPPLIES

G6/4mm crochet hook

Small amount of Worsted weight yarn

Ch 13.

Row 1: sc in 2nd ch from hook and in each remaining ch across (12 sts).

Fasten off. Coil strip into a ring following the natural curl of the piece. Sew ends together.

Weave in yarn tails.

Party Plate

Make a magic ring, ch 1.

Rnd 1: 6 sc in ring, pull ring closed tight, join with sl st to first st (6 sts).

Rnd 2: ch 1, 2 sc in each st around, join with sl st to first st. Place marker for beginning of rnd and move marker up as each rnd is completed (12 sts).

Rnd 3: ch 1, *sc in next st, 2 sc in next st* 6 times, join with sl st to first st (18 sts).

Rnd 4: ch 1, sc in next st, 2 sc in next st, *sc in next 2 sts, 2 sc in next st* 5 times, sc in next st, join with sl st to first st (24 sts).

Rnd 5: ch 1, *sc in next 3 sts, 2 sc in next st* 6 times, join with sl st to first st (30 sts).

Rnd 6: ch 1, sc in next 2 sts, 2 sc in next st, *sc in next 4 sts, 2 sc in next st* 5 times, sc in next 2 sts, join with sl st to first st (36 sts).

Rnd 7: ch 1, working in **front loops only**, *sc in next 5 sts, 2 sc in next st* 6 times, join with sl st to first st (42 sts).

Rnd 8: ch 1, working in **back loops only**, sc in next 3 sts, 2 sc in next st, *sc in next 6 sts, 2 sc in next st* 5 times, sc in next 3 sts, join with sl st to first st (48 sts).

Rnd 9: ch 1, resuming work in **both loops**, *sc in next 7 sts, 2 sc in next st* 6 times, join with sl st to first st (54 sts).

Fasten off. Weave in ends.

*The plates are worked in **joined rounds**. Staggered increases are key to their nice round shape. For the most rigid plates, choose a brand of yarn that is rather stiff. If more firmness is desired, the plates can be stiffened with diluted white glue (see page 41) or a commercial stiffening product.*

SUPPLIES

G6/4mm crochet hook

Small amount of Worsted weight yarn

Note: A chain 1 at the beginning of a round does not count as a stitch.

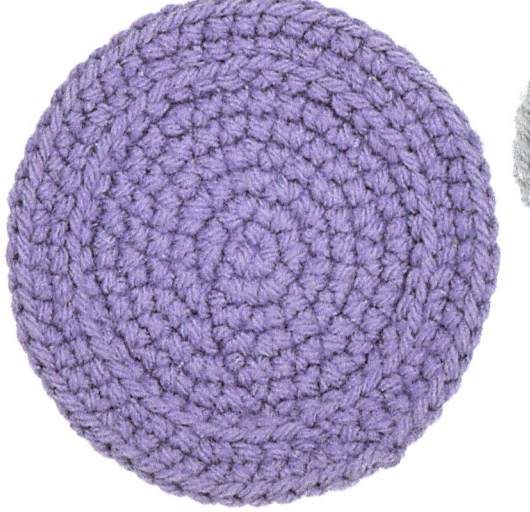

Serving Plate

Like the Party Plates, the Serving Plate is worked in **joined rounds**. A scalloped rim gives the plate a decorative edge. For the most rigid plate, choose a brand of yarn that is rather stiff. If more firmness is desired, the plate can be stiffened with diluted white glue (see page 41) or a commercial stiffening product.

SUPPLIES

G6/4mm crochet hook

Small amount of Worsted weight yarn

Note: A chain 1 at the beginning of a round does not count as a stitch.

Make a magic ring, ch 1.

Rnd 1: 6 sc in ring, pull ring closed tight, join with sl st to first st (6 sts).

Rnd 2: ch 1, 2 sc in each st around, join with sl st to first st. Place marker for beginning of rnd and move marker up as each rnd is completed (12 sts).

Rnd 3: ch 1, *sc in next st, 2 sc in next st* 6 times, join with sl st to first st (18 sts).

Rnd 4: ch 1, sc in next st, 2 sc in next st, *sc in next 2 sts, 2 sc in next st* 5 times, sc in next st, join with sl st to first st (24 sts).

Rnd 5: ch 1, *sc in next 3 sts, 2 sc in next st* 6 times, join with sl st to first st (30 sts).

Rnd 6: ch 1, sc in next 2 sts, 2 sc in next st, *sc in next 4 sts, 2 sc in next st* 5 times, sc in next 2 sts, join with sl st to first st (36 sts).

Rnd 7: ch 1, working in **front loops only**, *sc in next 5 sts, 2 sc in next st* 6 times, join with sl st to first st (42 sts).

Rnd 8: ch 1, working in **back loops only**, sc in next 3 sts, 2 sc in next st, *sc in next 6 sts, 2 sc in next st* 5 times, sc in next 3 sts, join with sl st to first st (48 sts).

Rnd 9: ch 1, for **scallops**, resuming work in **both loops**, *sl st in next st, sc in next st, hdc in next st, 3 dc in next st, hdc in next st, sc in next st* 6 times, sl st in next st (8 scallops).

Fasten off. Weave in ends.

47

2-Tier Pastry Plate

The Pastry Plate is a tea party essential — and a child's delight. Hardware sets in 2 sizes are sold on Etsy, Ebay and Amazon. I like the 'short' or 'mini' hardware for my 2-Tier plates. This makes a 2-Tier Pastry Plate that is about 7" tall. For 1-Tier plates, I use the handle from standard-size hardware.

To shop online for hardware sets, search on "cake plate hardware" or "cake stand hardware".

Cardboard circles provide the support for each amigurumi tier. Templates are provided on page 93. Large washers from the hardware store are added for a sturdy structure.

The Pastry Plate is easy to disassemble for storage.

SUPPLIES

G6/4mm crochet hook

Small amount of Worsted weight yarn

Small amount of corrugated cardboard (shipping box)

4 fender washers 1/4" x 1 1/4" (washers w/oversize outside dia)

Cake plate hardware

Glue (for cardboard, see page 11)

4 self-adhesive felt pads, 1/2" (optional)

UPPER TIER

Make a magic ring, ch 1.

Rnd 1: 6 sc in ring, pull ring closed *almost* tight leaving a 1/4" hole to accommodate hardware (6 sts).

Rnd 2: 2 sc in each st around. Place marker for beginning of rnd and move marker up as each rnd is completed (12 sts).

Rnd 3: *sc in next st, 2 sc in next st* 6 times (18 sts).

Rnd 4: *sc in next 2 sts, 2 sc in next st* 6 times (24 sts).

Rnd 5: *sc in next 3 sts, 2 sc in next st* 6 times (30 sts).

Rnd 6: *sc in next 4 sts, 2 sc in next st* 6 times (36 sts).

Rnd 7: *sc in next 5 sts, 2 sc in next st* 6 times (42 sts).

Rnd 8: *sc in next 6 sts, 2 sc in next st* 6 times (48 sts).

Rnd 9: for **scallops**, working in **back loops only**, *skip next st, 5 dc in next st, skip next st, sc in next st* 12 times (12 scallops).

Fasten off. Weave in ends.

LOWER TIER

Make a magic ring, ch 1.

Rnd 1: 6 sc in ring, pull ring closed *almost* tight leaving a 1/4" hole to accommodate hardware (6 sts).

Rnd 2: 2 sc in each st around. Place marker for beginning of rnd and move marker up as each rnd is completed (12 sts).

Rnd 3: *sc in next st, 2 sc in next st* 6 times (18 sts).

Rnd 4: *sc in next 2 sts, 2 sc in next st* 6 times (24 sts).

Rnd 5: *sc in next 3 sts, 2 sc in next st* 6 times (30 sts).

Rnd 6: *sc in next 4 sts, 2 sc in next st* 6 times (36 sts).

Rnd 7: *sc in next 5 sts, 2 sc in next st* 6 times (42 sts).

Rnd 8: *sc in next 6 sts, 2 sc in next st* 6 times (48 sts).

Rnd 9: *sc in next 7 sts, 2 sc in next st* 6 times (54 sts).

Rnd 10: *sc in next 8 sts, 2 sc in next st* 6 times (60 sts).

Rnd 11: for **scallops**, working in **back loops only**, *skip next st, 5 dc in next st, skip next st, sc in next st* 15 times (15 scallops).

Fasten off. Weave in ends.

1-Tier Pastry Plate

FINISHING

Using the templates on page 93, cut 2 circles from corrugated cardboard: one 3 1/2" in diameter and one 4 1/2" in diameter. Using a phillips screwdriver, poke a 1/4" hole in the centers.

Assemble the parts in this order: screw, fender washer, 4 1/2" cardboard circle, fender washer, ami lower tier, straight rod, small metal washer, fender washer, 3 1/2" cardboard circle, fender washer, ami upper tier, top handle.

For **stabilization pads**, cut four 1/2" circles or squares from corrugated cardboard. Glue to bottom of lower tier's cardboard circle at equal intervals. **Tip:** Self-adhesive felt pads can be used instead.

This variation of the pastry plate can be made using just the lower tier and a hardware handle.

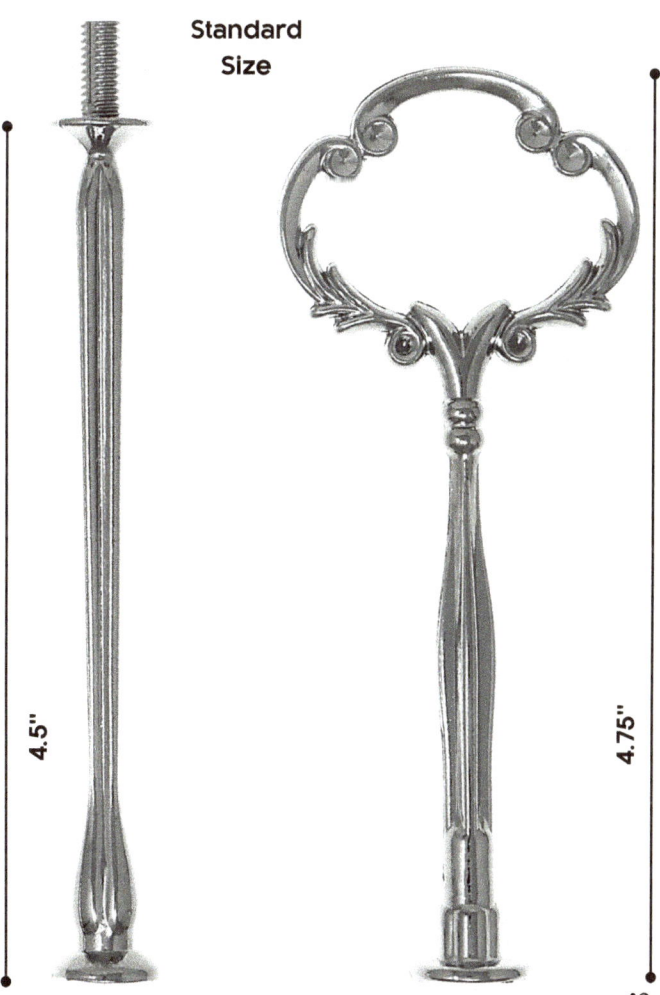

CAKE PLATE HARDWARE
Actual Size

Mini or Short Size — 2.75", 3.5"

Standard Size — 4.5", 4.75"

Vase of Flowers

A well-dressed table needs flowers and this little bouquet of Periwinkle is the perfect touch.

Place coins, beans, marbles or stones in the vase for weight (older kids only); or, make a weight by tying dry rice in a square of nylon stocking, tulle or saran wrap.

SUPPLIES

G6/4mm crochet hook

Small amount of Worsted weight yarn in purple, yellow & green

Small piece of lightweight cardboard (cereal box)

Floral stem wire, 22 gauge

Glue (for fabric, see page 11)

VASE

With yellow yarn, make a magic ring, ch 1.

Rnd 1: 6 sc in ring, pull ring closed tight (6 sts).

Rnd 2: 2 sc in each st around. Place marker for beginning of rnd and move marker up as each rnd is completed (12 sts).

Rnd 3: *sc in next st, 2 sc in next st* 6 times (18 sts).

Rnd 4: *sc in next 2 sts, 2 sc in next st* 6 times (24 sts).

Rnd 5: *sc in next 3 sts, 2 sc in next st* 6 times (30 sts).

Rnd 6: working in **back loops only**, sc in each st around.

Rnd 7: resuming work in **both loops**, *sc in next 4 sts, sc2tog* 5 times (25 sts).

Cut a circle of cardboard 1 3/4" diameter (see template, page 93) and place on top of Rnd 7.

Rnds 8-10: sc in each st around.

Rnd 11: *sc in next 3 sts, sc2tog* 5 times (20 sts).

Rnds 11-14: sc in each st around.

Rnd 15: *sc in next 3 sts, sc2tog* 4 times (16 sts).

Rnds 16-17: sc in each st around.

Rnd 18: *sc in next 6 sts, sc2tog* 2 times (14 sts).

Rnds 19-20: sc in each st around.

Rnd 21: *sc in next st, 2 sc in next st* 7 times (21 sts).

Sl st in next st. Fasten off. Weave in ends.

FLOWERS (MAKE 5)

With purple yarn, make a magic ring, ch 1.

Rnd 1: 5 sc in ring, pull ring closed tight (5 sts).

Rnds 2-3: for **base**, sc in each st around; push down on Rnd 1 with handle of crochet hook to make a cup shape.

Rnd 4: for **petals**, (sl st, ch 2, 2 dc, ch 2, sl st) in each st around (5 petals).

Sl st in next st. Fasten off.

STEMS (MAKE 5)

For **center of flower**, cut two 5-inch pieces of yellow yarn. Fold a 12" piece of floral stem wire in half and knot the double-strand of yellow yarn around fold (see Fig. A). Separate yarn plies with pointed tip of needle and trim to 1/2" (see Fig. B).

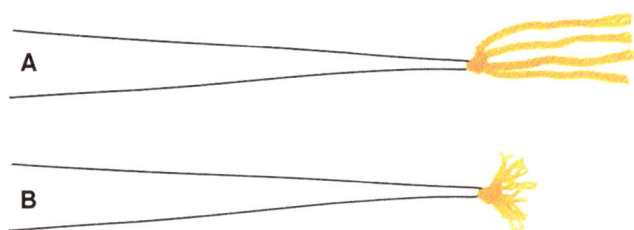

Apply glue to yellow knot, pinch legs of stem wire together to close the gap, and insert down thru center of flower. Pull wire until knot rests snugly against base.

Twist legs of wire together and trim stem to desired length.

Wrap stem: Knot green yarn around top of stem and sew tail securely into base. Coil yarn around-and-around stem. This goes quickly if you spin the stem between your fingertips. Secure end with a dab of glue.

Hide remaining yarn tails inside base.

How to Set the Table

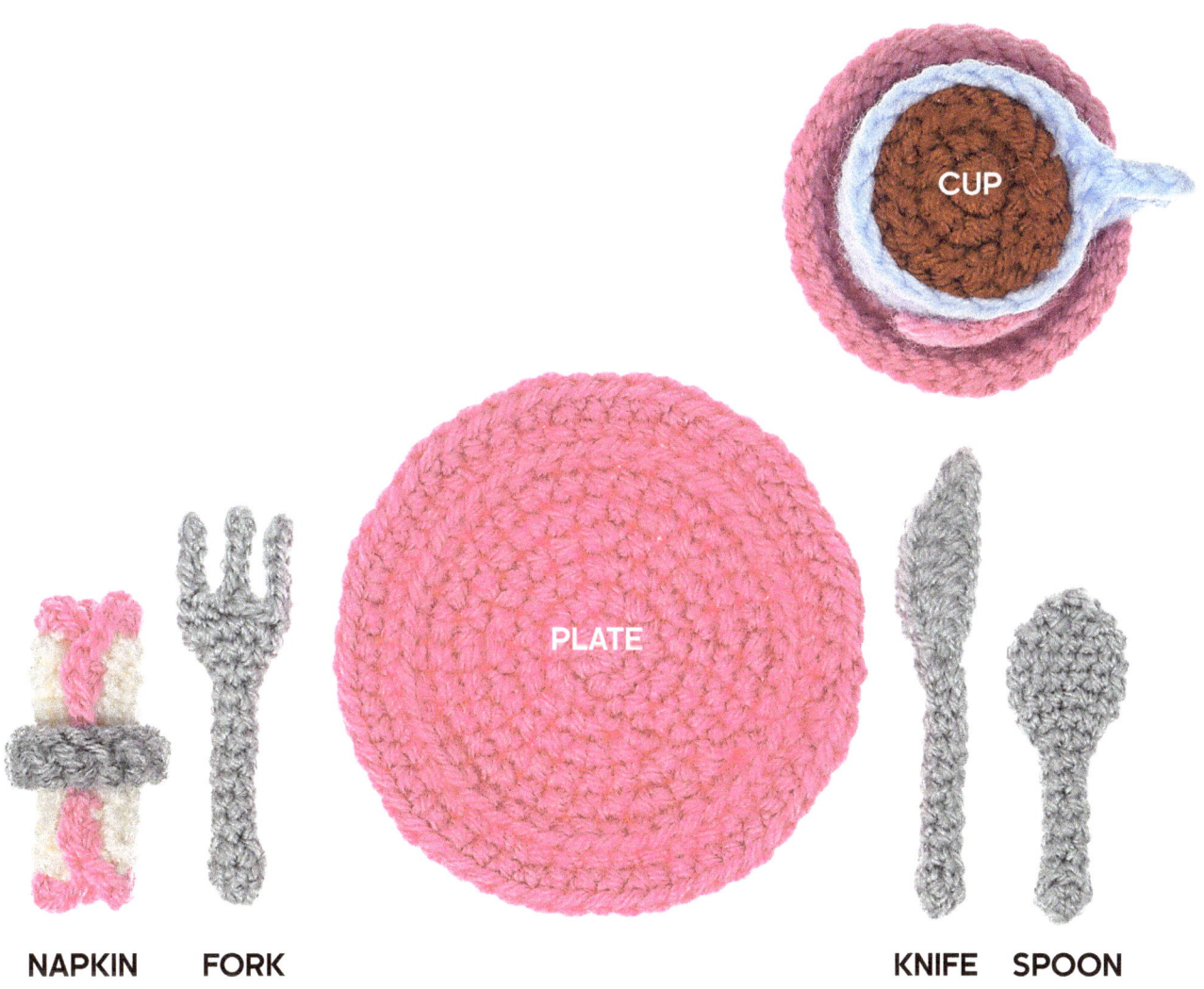

Tea Bag

Cinnamon Roll

SUPPLIES

E4/3.5mm crochet hook

Small amount of DK, Light Worsted yarn in rust, off-white, gray and green

Glue (for fabric, see page 11)

BAG

The bag is worked around a foundation chain.

With rust yarn, ch 5.

Rnd 1: sc in 2nd ch from hook, sc in next 2 chs, 3 sc in last ch, working around other side of chain, sc in next 3 chs, 2 sc in last ch (11 sts).

Rnds 2-4: sc in each st around; change to off-white yarn in last st of Rnd 4.

Rnd 5: sc in each st around.

Rnd 6: sc in next 10 sts, skip last st (10 sts).

Rnd 7: sc in next 5 sts, skip next st, sc in next 4 sts (9 sts). Fasten off with extra long tail.

Using yarn tail, sew end of bag closed — then knot tail at center of edge to be used for tea bag's string. Embroider a gray stitch at top of bag as shown in picture.

TAG (MAKE 2)

With green yarn, make a magic ring, ch 1.

Rnd 1: 4 sc in ring, pull ring closed tight (4 sts).

Rnd 2: 3 sc in each st around (12 sts). Fasten off.

Weave string of tea bag into back of one tag and adjust so that string is about 4" long. Knot string to starting tail of tag. Cut remaining tails short. Glue both tags together with wrong sides facing and yarn tails sandwiched between. Push tags into a square shape before glue dries.

This pattern can be worked in other color combinations to make pinwheel cookies.

SUPPLIES

E4/3.5mm crochet hook

Small amount of DK, Light Worsted yarn in tan and brown

Glue (for fabric, see page 11)

OUTER STRIPE

With tan yarn, loosely ch 42.

Row 1: dc in 3rd ch from hook and in each remaining ch across (40 sts). Fasten off.

INNER STRIPE

With brown yarn, loosely ch 32.

Row 1: dc in 3rd ch from hook and in each remaining ch across (30 sts). Fasten off.

FINISHING

Starting with ends of stripes that don't have tails, lay inner stripe on top of outer stripe offset 1/2" from end. Roll stripes into a coil as shown in picture. Insert pins in edge to hold cinnamon roll in position while you finish it up.

Secure loose ends of stripes by sewing them to the adjacent coil with whip stitches; then sew yarn tails back and forth thru diameter several times to hold the shape.

For further reinforcement, insert tip of glue bottle randomly between coils and apply glue.

Frosted Donut

The easy donut is worked in rows, then sewn into a ring. Instructions are provided for a donut with blue frosting — but frosted donuts are at their best when made in lots of different colors!

SUPPLIES

E4/3.5mm

Small amount of DK, Light Worsted yarn in tan and blue

Bugle beads in assorted colors, 6mm

Glue (for beads, see page 11)

Polyester fiberfill stuffing

Note: A chain 1 at the beginning of a row is for turning your work and does not count as a stitch.

With tan yarn, ch 12.

Row 1: ch 1, turn, sc in each st across (12 sts).

Row 2: ch 1, turn, 2 sc in each st across (24 sts).

Rows 3-4: ch 1, turn, sc in each st across; change to blue yarn in last st of Row 4.

Row 5: ch 1, turn, sc in each st across.

Row 6: ch 1, turn, sc2tog 12 times (12 sts).

Fasten off.

The piece should now look like a letter C. Sew the 12 sts of Rows 1 and 6 together stitch-by-stitch with blue yarn tail to make a tube.

Stuff the tube by pushing fiberfill into each end. Long craft tweezers are ideal for this.

Bend the C into an O. Sew ends together using tan yarn tail to sew tan area — and blue yarn tail to sew blue area. Hide yarn tails inside.

Glue bugle beads randomly to frosting.

Macaron

The macaron is made in 3 separate pieces that are glued together. A final round of slip stitch on the filling adds thickness to the rim. Macarons provide a marvelous opportunity to play with color. Use the photos for inspiration!

SUPPLIES

E4/3.5mm crochet hook

Small amount of DK, Light Worsted yarn in assorted colors

Glue (for fabric, see page 11)

COOKIE (MAKE 2)

Make a magic ring, ch 1.

Rnd 1: 6 sc in ring, pull ring closed tight (6 sts).

Rnd 2: 2 sc in each st around. Place marker for beginning of rnd and move marker up as each rnd is completed (12 sts).

Rnd 3: *sc in next st, 2 sc in next st* 6 times (18 sts).

Rnd 4: sc in each st around.

Rnd 5: working in **back loops only**, *sc in next st, sc2tog* 6 times, join with sl st in first st (12 sts).

Rnd 6: ch 1, resuming work in **both loops**, sc2tog 6 times (6 sts).

Fasten off. With craft tweezers, stuff **starting tail** inside cookie. Thread **ending tail** onto needle, insert needle thru front loop of each st around opening and pull tight to close hole. Trim tail to 1/2".

FILLING

Make a magic ring, ch 1.

Rnd 1: 6 sc in ring, pull ring closed tight (6 sts).

Rnd 2: 2 sc in each st around. Place marker for beginning of rnd and move marker up as each rnd is completed (12 sts).

Rnd 3: *sc in next st, 2 sc in next st* 6 times (18 sts).

Rnd 4: sl st in each st around.

Fasten off.

FINISHING

Glue cookies to filling as shown in picture.

Chocolate Chip Cookie

*Seed beads are used for the chocolate chips. I found small packs on Etsy that were perfect. Search on "6/0 czech seed beads **brown**".*

SUPPLIES

E4/3.5mm crochet hook

Small amount of DK, Light Worsted yarn in tan

Seed beads in brown, 6/0

Glue (for beads, see page 11) or sewing thread & beading needle

Make a magic ring, ch 1.

Rnd 1: 6 sc in ring, pull ring closed tight (6 sts).

Rnd 2: 2 sc in each st around. Place marker for beginning of rnd and move marker up as each rnd is completed (12 sts).

Rnd 3: *sc in next st, 2 sc in next st* 6 times (18 sts).

Rnd 4: sc in next st, 2 sc in next st, *sc in next 2 sts, 2 sc in next st* 5 times, sc in next st (24 sts).

Rnd 5: sc in each st around.

Rnd 6: sc in next st, sc2tog, *sc in next 2 sts, sc2tog* 5 times, sc in next st (18 sts).

Rnd 7: *sc in next st, sc2tog* 6 times (12 sts).

Rnd 8: sc2tog 6 times (6 sts).

Fasten off. With craft tweezers, stuff **starting tail** inside the cookie. Thread **ending tail** onto needle, insert needle thru front loop of each stitch around opening and pull tight to close hole. Flatten into cookie shape. Hide yarn tail inside.

Beads: Glue or sew beads to top of cookie as shown in photo. If sewing, hide your sts in grooves between rnds.

Candy Cookie

*Seed beads in assorted colors are used for the candies. I found small packs of multicolor beads on Etsy. Search on "6/0 czech seed beads **color mix**".*

SUPPLIES

E4/3.5mm crochet hook

Small amount of DK, Light Worsted yarn in tan

Seed beads in assorted colors, 6/0

Glue (for beads, see page 11) or sewing thread & beading needle

Make the same as Chocolate Chip Cookie.

Create-a-Cupcake

SUPPLIES

E4/3.5mm crochet hook

Small amount of DK, Light Worsted yarn in assorted colors

Neodymium disc magnets, N35 (strength), 12mm x 2mm (size)

Small amount of felt

Glue (for fabric, see page 11)

Super glue or Gorilla Glue (for magnets)

Polyester fiberfill stuffing

★ CRAFTING WITH MAGNETS

All magnets have north and south poles. Opposite poles attract each other, while the same poles repel each other. In order for your cupcakes to be mix-and-match, all cakes must have the same pole facing UP (e.g. north) and all frosting pieces must have the opposite pole facing DOWN (e.g. south). Using a pen that will write on metal (e.g. Sharpie), take your stack of magnets and mark all upward facing sides with an X. This makes it easy to identify poles that are the same.

Create-a-Cupcake was designed with interchangeable parts...and the magic of magnets. The cake, cupcake paper and frosting are 3 separate pieces to assemble for creative play. The cake tucks into the cupcake paper — and the frosting adheres to the cake with magnets. It's such fun when the cake grabs the frosting! Pretend-chefs can make cupcakes in countless color combinations. Shop for magnets at hardware stores, craft stores, amazon or ebay.

Cake   Cupcake Paper   Frosting

For the best fit, use the same brand of yarn for everything. The cake should fit snugly in the cupcake paper. If it's too loose or too tight, go down or up a hook size.

Flavor ideas for your cakes include chocolate, vanilla, strawberry, lemon, carrot, red velvet and green velvet. Have fun making all components in lots of different colors!

Tip: For no-magnet cupcakes, simply glue your frosting to the cake. Kids will still have the fun of mixing-and-matching their cakes to the cupcake papers.

CAKE

The cake is worked from top to bottom.

Make a magic ring, ch 1.

Rnd 1: 6 sc in ring, pull ring closed tight (6 sts).

Rnd 2: 2 sc in each st around. Place marker for beginning of rnd and move marker up as each rnd is completed (12 sts).

Rnd 3: *sc in next st, 2 sc in next st* 6 times (18 sts).

Rnd 4: *sc in next 2 sts, 2 sc in next st* 6 times (24 sts).

Insert magnet: On wrong side of cake, attach X side of magnet to center of Rnd 1 as follows. Apply a drop of **super glue** to center of magnet and press it firmly onto fabric. Let dry 24 hours.

Rnds 5-6: sc in each st around.

Rnd 7: *sc in next 2 sts, sc2tog* 6 times (18 sts).

Rnds 8-9: sc in each st around.

Rnd 10: working in **back loops only**, sc in each st around.

Rnd 11: resuming work in **both loops**, *sc in next st, sc2tog* 6 times (12 sts).

Stuff the cake.

Rnd 12: sc2tog 6 times (6 sts).

Fasten off with extra long tail.

Finish adding stuffing. Thread ending tail onto needle, insert needle thru front loop of each stitch around opening and pull tight to close hole. Use remaining yarn tail to **shape the cake** as follows: Sew up and down thru cake several times avoiding magnet and pulling on yarn gently to compress cake and create a flat bottom with a domed top. Continue until you get a nice shape. Hide yarn tail inside.

CUPCAKE PAPER

Make a magic ring, ch 1.

Rnd 1: 6 sc in ring, pull ring closed tight (6 sts).

Rnd 2: 2 sc in each st around. Place marker for beginning of rnd and move marker up as each rnd is completed (12 sts).

Rnd 3: *sc in next st, 2 sc in next st* 6 times (18 sts).

Rnd 4: working in **back loops only**, sc in each st around (18 sts).

Rnd 5: resuming work in **both loops**, *sc in next 2 sts, 2 sc in next st* 6 times (24 sts).

Rnds 6-7: sc in each st around.

Rnd 8: *sc in next 3 sts, 2 sc in next st* 6 times (30 sts).

Rnd 9: sc in each st around.

Sl st in next st. Fasten off. Weave in end.

FROSTING

Make a magic ring, ch 1.

Rnd 1: 6 sc in ring, pull ring closed tight (6 sts).

Rnd 2: 2 sc in each st around. Place marker for beginning of rnd and move marker up as each rnd is completed (12 sts).

Rnd 3: *sc in next st, 2 sc in next st* 6 times (18 sts).

Rnd 4: sc in each st around.

Rnd 5: *sc in next 5 sts, 2 sc in next st* 3 times (21 sts).

Rnd 6: for **scallops**, *5 sc in next st, skip 1 st, sl st in next st* 7 times (7 scallops).

Fasten off. Weave in end. Cut starting tail to 1/2".

Attach magnet: On wrong side of frosting, glue X side of magnet to center of Rnd 1 by applying a drop of **super glue** to center of magnet and pressing it firmly onto fabric. Let dry 24 hours.

Cover magnet: Using a coin for a pattern, cut a circle of felt slightly larger than magnet. Apply **fabric glue** to perimeter of circle and glue felt to frosting so magnet is encased.

Magnet   Felt Cover

CHERRY

For a video demo of making hdc sts in a magic ring, visit my Amigurumi Tutorials board on Pinterest (see page 89) or browse YouTube.

Make a magic ring, ch 1.

Rnd 1: 5 hdc in ring, pull ring closed tight (5 sts).

Fasten off. Push on center of Rnd 1 with handle of crochet hook to pop cherry into shape. Knot yarn tails together and thread them onto yarn needle. Push needle up into cherry and out thru center of Rnd 1. Glue cherry to top of frosting. Trim yarn tails flush with cherry.

Petit Fours

A petit four is a tiny cake and a tea party classic. Three garnishes are provided.

★ SC3TOG USED IN THIS PATTERN
(Insert hook in next st and pull up a loop) **3 times**, yarn over and pull through all 4 loops on hook

SUPPLIES

E4/3.5mm crochet hook

Small amount of DK, Light Worsted yarn in assorted colors

Glue (for fabric, see page 11)

Polyester fiberfill stuffing

CAKE

Make a magic ring, ch 1.

Rnd 1: 4 sc in ring, pull ring closed tight (4 sts).

Rnd 2: 3 sc in each st around. Place marker for beginning of rnd and move marker up as each rnd is completed (12 sts).

Rnd 3: sc in next st, 3 sc in next st, *sc in next 2 sts, 3 sc in next st* 3 times, sc in next st (20 sts).

Rnd 4: working in **back loops only**, sc in each st around.

Rnds 5-8: resuming work in **both loops**, sc in each st around.

Rnd 9: working in **back loops only**, sc in next st, sc3tog, *sc in next 2 sts, sc3tog* 3 times, sc in next st (12 sts).

Stuff the cake.

Rnd 10: resuming work in **both loops**, sc3tog 4 times (4 sts).

Fasten off with extra long tail.

Thread ending tail onto needle, insert needle thru front loop of each stitch around opening and pull tight to close hole. Use remaining yarn tail to **shape the cake** as follows: Sew up and down thru cake several times pulling on yarn very gently to compress the cake and create a flat top and bottom. Hide yarn tail inside.

GARNISHES

BOW

Cut a piece of contrasting yarn and tie in a bow around cake like you are wrapping a gift box. Trim tails short as shown in picture. Glue bow against surface of cake.

ROSEBUD & LEAVES

For **rosebud**, make a magic ring, ch 1.

Rnd 1: 5 hdc in ring, pull ring closed tight. Fasten off.

Knot tails together. Push handle of crochet hook into center of Rnd 1 to pop rosebud into shape.

For **1st leaf**, ch 3.

Row 1: sl st in 2nd ch from hook, sc in next st (2 sts).

Do not fasten off.

Row 2: for **2nd leaf**, ch 3, sl st in 2nd ch from hook, sc in next st (2 sts).

Fasten off. Pinch tips of leaves into points.

Finishing: Position leaves and rosebud on top of cake. Sew their tails down thru top of cake and out the bottom. Glue garnish in place. Trim tails flush with surface of cake.

ZIG ZAG

Embroider with contrasting yarn.

1. Leaving a 6-inch starting tail, push needle up thru bottom of cake and out the top at A.

Note: Steps 2-4 are long stitches made thru top layer only.

2. Push needle in at B and out at C

3. Push needle in at D and out at E

4. Push needle in at D and out at B

5. Push needle in at C and out at bottom of cake in exact spot where starting tail began.

Knot tails together.

Thread needle with tails and hide them inside cake.

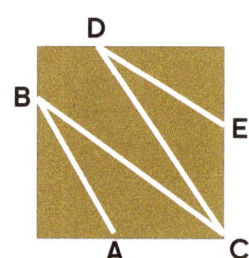

Heart Sandwich Cookie

These cookies are small and dainty, but also sturdy due to glued layers. The entire heart is worked into a magic ring in 1 round. When you pull the ring closed tight, the heart takes shape like magic!

If you need to see a demo of how to dc and tr in a magic ring, videos are available on YouTube. Visit the Amigurumi Tutorials board on my Pinterest page to see my favorites (see page 89) or search directly on YouTube.

SUPPLIES

E4/3.5mm crochet hook

Small amount of DK, Light Worsted yarn in purple & white

Glue (for fabric, see page 11)

HEART (MAKE 3)

Make 2 in purple and 1 in white.

All sts except the chs are worked into a magic ring.

Make a magic ring, ch 3.

Rnd 1: 3 tr, 3 dc, tr, 3 dc, 3 tr, ch 3, sl st. Pull ring closed tight. Fasten off.

Knot tails together and trim ends to 1/2". Glue wrong sides of purple hearts to white heart.

Thumbprint Cookie

Pearlized buttons are used for the cookie's jelly center. I purchased the buttons pictured on Etsy.

SUPPLIES

E4/3.5mm crochet hook

Small amount of DK, Light Worsted yarn in tan

Pearlized shank button in red, 9/16" diameter

Sewing thread

Make a magic ring, ch 1.

Rnd 1: 6 sc in ring, pull ring closed tight (6 sts).

Rnd 2: 2 sc in each st around. Place marker for beginning of rnd and move marker up as each rnd is completed (12 sts).

Rnd 3: *sc in next st, 2 sc in next st* 6 times (18 sts).

Rnd 4: sc in each st around.

Rnd 5: *sc in next st, sc2tog* 6 times (12 sts).

Rnd 6: sc2tog 6 times (6 sts).

Fasten off. Thread ending tail onto needle, insert needle thru front loop of each stitch around opening and pull tight to close hole. Flatten into cookie shape. Hide yarn tail inside. Sew button to middle of cookie.

Rainbow Stack-a-Cake

The Rainbow Stack-a-Cake is great fun for play. Young chefs can 'bake' the colorful cake layers, top them with frosting and stack them into a grand creation. Tea Party guests will receive a frosted layer when the cake is served.

The cake isn't stuffed, so I like to use a lofty yarn. It's important for the diameter of all cake and frosting layers to match. Even within the same yarn brand, the strand thickness can vary among colors and cause size variance. If you find that your disks aren't consistent in size, adjust as needed by using a different size hook. I found this easy by crocheting all of my layers thru Rnd 5, stacking them to compare sizes and tweaking if needed.

SUPPLIES

G6/4mm crochet hook

Small amount of Worsted weight yarn in pink, orange, yellow, green, turquoise, purple and cream

Bugle beads in assorted colors, 6mm

Glue (for beads, see page 11)

CAKE LAYERS (MAKE 6)

Make each layer a different color as shown in picture.

Make a magic ring, ch 1.

Rnd 1: 6 sc in ring, pull ring closed tight (6 sts).

Rnd 2: 2 sc in each st around. Place marker for beginning of rnd and move marker up as each rnd is completed (12 sts).

Rnd 3: *sc in next st, 2 sc in next st* 6 times (18 sts).

Rnd 4: sc in next st, 2 sc in next st, *sc in next 2 sts, 2 sc in next st* 5 times, sc in next st (24 sts).

Rnd 5: *sc in next 3 sts, 2 sc in next st* 6 times (30 sts).

Rnd 6: sc in each st around.

Rnd 7: *sc in next 3 sts, sc2tog* 6 times (24 sts).

Rnd 8: sc in next st, sc2tog, *sc in next 2 sts, sc2tog* 5 times, sc in next st (18 sts).

Rnd 9: *sc in next st, sc2tog* 6 times (12 sts).

Rnd 10: sc2tog 6 times (6 sts).

Fasten off. Thread ending tail onto needle, insert needle thru front loop of each stitch around opening and pull tight to close hole. Flatten into shape. The disk should be flat for stacking. If your disk bulges in the middle, sew up and down thru both layers at center several times until bulge is eliminated. Hide end inside.

FROSTING LAYERS (MAKE 6)

With cream yarn, make a magic ring, ch 1.

Rnd 1: 6 sc in ring, pull ring closed tight (6 sts).

Rnd 2: 2 sc in each st around. Place marker for beginning of rnd and move marker up as each rnd is completed (12 sts).

Rnd 3: *sc in next st, 2 sc in next st* 6 times (18 sts).

Rnd 4: sc in next st, 2 sc in next st, *sc in next 2 sts, 2 sc in next st* 5 times, sc in next st (24 sts).

Rnd 5: *sc in next 3 sts, 2 sc in next st* 6 times (30 sts).

Rnd 6: sl st in each st around.

Fasten off. Weave in ends.

FINISHING

Glue beads to one frosting layer. Stack layers as shown in picture.

Chocolate Strawberry Stack-a-Cake

The Chocolate Strawberry Stack-a-Cake is made the same as the Rainbow version. Refer to the Rainbow Stack-a-Cake for tips on obtaining same-size layers.

SUPPLIES

G6/4mm and E4/3.5mm crochet hooks

Small amount of Worsted weight yarn in brown and cream

Small amount of DK, Light Worsted yarn in red and green

Glue (for fabric, see page 11)

Polyester fiberfill stuffing

CAKE LAYERS (MAKE 3)

With Worsted weight yarn in brown and G6/4mm crochet hook, make the same as cake layers for Rainbow Stack-a-Cake.

FROSTING LAYERS (MAKE 3)

With Worsted weight yarn in cream and G6/4mm crochet hook, make the same as frosting layers for Rainbow Stack-a-Cake.

STRAWBERRY

With DK, Light Worsted yarn in red and E4/3.5mm crochet hook, make a magic ring, ch 1.

Rnd 1: 7 sc in ring, pull ring closed tight (7 sts).

Rnd 2: sc in each st around.

Rnd 3: 2 sc in each st around (14 sts).

Rnds 4-5: sc in each st around.

Rnd 6: sc2tog 7 times (7 sts).

Fasten off. Stuff strawberry. Thread ending tail onto needle, insert needle thru front loop of each stitch around opening and pull tight to close hole. Hide end inside.

STRAWBERRY LEAVES

With DK, Light Worsted yarn in green and E4/3.5mm crochet hook, make a magic ring, ch 1.

Rnd 1: 5 sc in ring, pull ring closed tight (5 sts).

Rnd 2: *sl st in next st, ch 5, sl st in same st as where your ch started* 5 times (5 leaves).

Fasten off. Sew or glue leaves to top of strawberry.

FINISHING

Glue strawberry to one frosting layer. Stack layers as shown in photo.

Fruit Tart

The crust and filling of the fruit tart are made as 2 separate pieces. Kids can 'bake' the crust before the filling is added.

Seed beads are used for the kiwi seeds. Craft tweezers are ideal for stuffing the strawberry and blueberry.

SUPPLIES

G6/4mm crochet hook and E4/3.5mm crochet hooks

Small amount of Worsted weight yarn in honey and cream

Small amount of DK, Light Worsted yarn in red, orange, blue, light green and bright green

Seed beads in black, 10/0

Glue (for fabric & beads, see page 11)

Sewing thread & beading needle (optional)

Polyester fiberfill stuffing

CRUST

With Worsted weight yarn in honey and G6/4mm crochet hook, make a magic ring, ch 1.

Rnd 1: 6 sc in ring, pull ring closed tight (6 sts).

Rnd 2: 2 sc in each st around. Place marker for beginning of rnd and move marker up as each rnd is completed (12 sts).

Rnd 3: *sc in next st, 2 sc in next st* 6 times (18 sts).

Rnd 4: *sc in next 2 sts, 2 sc in next st* 6 times (24 sts).

Rnd 5: *sc in next 3 sts, 2 sc in next st* 6 times (30 sts).

Rnd 6: *sc in next 4 sts, 2 sc in next st* 6 times (36 sts).

Rnd 7: ch 1, turn, working in **front loops only**, sc in each st around.

Rnds 8-9: resuming work in **both loops**, sc in each st around.

Rnd 10: for **fluted edge**, *sl st in next st, ch 2* around. Sl st in next st. Fasten off. Weave in ends.

FILLING

With Worsted weight yarn in cream and G6/4mm crochet hook, make a magic ring, ch 1.

Rnd 1: 6 sc in ring, pull ring closed tight (6 sts).

Rnd 2: 2 sc in each st around. Place marker for beginning of rnd and move marker up as each rnd is completed (12 sts).

Rnd 3: *sc in next st, 2 sc in next st* 6 times (18 sts).

Rnd 4: sc in next st, 2 sc in next st, *sc in next 2 sts, 2 sc in next st* 5 times, sc in next st (24 sts).

Rnd 5: *sc in next 3 sts, 2 sc in next st* 6 times (30 sts).

Rnd 6: sc in next 2 sts, 2 sc in next st, *sc in next 4 sts, 2 sc in next st* 5 times, sc in next 2 sts (36 sts).

Rnd 7: sc in each st around.

Rnd 8: sc in next 2 sts, sc2tog, *sc in next 4 sts, sc2tog* 5 times, sc in next 2 sts (30 sts).

Rnd 9: *sc in next 3 sts, sc2tog* 6 times (24 sts).

Rnd 10: sc in next st, sc2tog, *sc in next 2 sts, sc2tog* 5 times, sc in next st (18 sts).

Rnd 11: *sc in next st, sc2tog* 6 times (12 sts).

Add a small amount of stuffing if needed. I used a lofty yarn (see page 91) and my filling was a perfect fit for the crust without any stuffing.

Rnd 12: sc2tog 6 times (6 sts).

Fasten off. Thread ending tail onto needle, insert needle thru front loop of each stitch around opening and pull tight to close hole. Hide end inside.

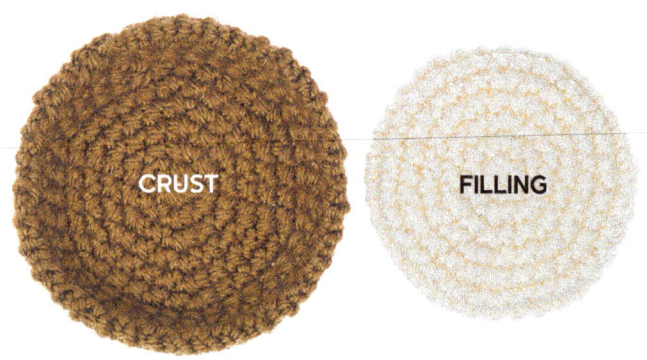

TANGERINE

With DK, Light Worsted yarn in orange and E4/3.5mm crochet hook, make a magic ring, ch 1.

Rnd 1: 6 sc in ring, pull ring closed tight (6 sts).

Rnd 2: 2 sc in each st around. Place marker for beginning of rnd & move marker up as each rnd is completed (12 sts).

Rnd 3: 2 sc in each st around (24 sts).

Fold in half with wrong sides facing.

Row 4: ch 1, sl st thru both layers along open edge to close up the tangerine segment.

Fasten off. Hide end inside.

STRAWBERRY

With DK, Light Worsted yarn in red and E4/3.5mm crochet hook, make a magic ring, ch 1.

Rnd 1: 7 sc in ring, pull ring closed tight (7 sts).

Rnd 2: sc in each st around. Place marker for beginning of rnd and move marker up as each rnd is completed.

Rnd 3: 2 sc in each st around (14 sts).

Rnds 4-5: sc in each st around.

Rnd 6: sc2tog 7 times (7 sts).

Fasten off. Stuff berry. Thread ending tail onto needle, insert needle thru front loop of each stitch around opening and pull tight to close hole. Hide end inside.

KIWI

With DK, Light Worsted yarn in light green and E4/3.5mm crochet hook, make a magic ring, ch 1.

Rnd 1: 6 sc in ring, pull ring closed tight (6 sts).

Rnd 2: 2 sc in each st around; change to bright green yarn in last st. Place marker for beginning of rnd and move marker up as each rnd is completed (12 sts).

Rnd 3: *sc in next st, 2 sc in next st* 6 times (18 sts).

Rnd 4: sc in next st, 2 sc in next st, *sc in next 2 sts, 2 sc in next st* 5 times, sc in next st (24 sts).

Rnd 5: *sc in next 3 sts, 2 sc in next st* 6 times (30 sts).

Pause to glue or sew seed beads in groove between Rnds 2-3 and 3-4. Fold circle in half so that wrong sides face and stuff yarn tails inside.

Row 6: ch 1, sl st thru both layers along open edge to close up the kiwi slice.

Fasten off. Hide end inside.

BLUEBERRY

With DK, Light Worsted yarn in blue and E4/3.5mm crochet hook, leave a 6" starting tail, make a magic ring, ch 1.

Rnd 1: 6 sc in ring, pull ring closed tight (6 sts).

Rnd 2: *sc in next st, 2 sc in next st* 3 times. Place marker for beginning of rnd and move marker up as each rnd is completed (9 sts).

Rnd 3: sc in each st around.

Rnd 4: *sc in next st, sc2tog* 3 times (6 sts).

Fasten off. Stuff blueberry with starting tail. Thread ending tail onto needle, insert needle thru front loop of each stitch around opening and pull tight to close hole. Hide end inside.

FINISHING

Glue fruit to filling as shown in picture.

63

Strawberries

Patterns are provided for strawberries in 2 sizes. Make them for garnishes and strawberry tea.

SUPPLIES

E4/3.5mm crochet hook

Small amount of DK, Light Worsted yarn in red and green

Glue (for fabric, see page 11), optional

Polyester fiberfill stuffing

LARGE STRAWBERRY

With red yarn, make a magic ring, ch 1.

Rnd 1: 6 sc in ring, pull ring closed tight (6 sts).

Rnd 2: *sc in next st, 2 sc in next st* 3 times. Place marker for beginning of rnd and move marker up as each rnd is completed (9 sts).

Rnd 3: *sc in next 2 sts, 2 sc in next st* 3 times (12 sts).

Rnd 4: *sc in next 3 sts, 2 sc in next st* 3 times (15 sts).

Rnd 5: *sc in next 4 sts, 2 sc in next st* 3 times (18 sts).

Rnd 6: sc in each st around.

Rnd 7: *sc in next st, sc2tog* 6 times (12 sts).

Stuff the strawberry.

Rnd 8: sc2tog 6 times (6 sts).

Fasten off. Thread ending tail onto needle, insert needle thru front loop of each stitch around opening and pull tight to close hole. Hide end inside.

LEAVES

With green yarn, make a magic ring, ch 1.

Rnd 1: 6 sc in ring, pull ring closed tight (6 sts).

Rnd 2: *sl st in next st, ch 8, sl st in same st as where your ch started* 6 times (6 leaves).

Fasten off. Sew or glue leaves to top of strawberry.

SMALL STRAWBERRY

With DK, Light Worsted yarn in red and E4/3.5mm crochet hook, make a magic ring, ch 1.

Rnd 1: 7 sc in ring, pull ring closed tight (7 sts).

Rnd 2: sc in each st around.

Rnd 3: 2 sc in each st around (14 sts).

Rnds 4-5: sc in each st around.

Rnd 6: sc2tog 7 times (7 sts).

Fasten off. Stuff strawberry. Thread ending tail onto needle, insert needle thru front loop of each stitch around opening and pull tight to close hole. Hide end inside.

LEAVES

With DK, Light Worsted yarn in green and E4/3.5mm crochet hook, make a magic ring, ch 1.

Rnd 1: 5 sc in ring, pull ring closed tight (5 sts).

Rnd 2: *sl st in next st, ch 5, sl st in same st as where your ch started* 5 times (5 leaves).

Fasten off. Sew or glue leaves to top of strawberry.

HOT STRAWBERRY TEA

Add a strawberry to a cup of your favorite tea.

Top with sugar and cream.

Charlotte's Oven

The frame of Charlotte's enchanting oven is made from foam board, also known as foam core. You can find it at craft, art and office supply stores. It is most common to find it in white, but colors are also available. Your amigurumi pieces will be glued on top of the foam board.

The same magnets used for the Create-a-Cupcake pattern are used for the oven's door latch. Crafting Glue Dots are used for securely adhering the magnets and washers to the oven's frame.

A purchased cabinet pull is featured for the door handle. You will need to buy shorter screws for your  cabinet pull than the ones it includes. The cabinet pull shown is Amerock BP341626 from Home Depot, Amazon or Ace Hardware. Mine was painted yellow with spray enamel. Fender washers reinforce the cabinet pull area.

Buttons are used for the oven knobs. A weighted base keeps the oven steady when the door is opened.

SIZE: ~ 6" wide x 6" tall x 5" deep

Note: A chain 1 at the beginning of a row is for turning your work and does not count as a stitch.

SUPPLIES

G6/4mm crochet hook

Small amount of Worsted weight yarn in pink, green, purple, light gray & charcoal

Foam board or foam core, 20" x 30" x 3/16"

5 buttons, 5/8" diameter

Arch cabinet pull, 3" hole-to-hole (~4" total length)

2 machine screws to fit your cabinet pull, 1/2" long
Note: #8-32 is the standard size for U.S. cabinet-pull screws. The screws used for the cabinet pull pictured are size 8-32 x 1/2.

2 flat washers, 1/4" inner dia x 9/16" outer dia, steel (**not stainless steel**)

2 fender washers, 3/16" inner dia x 1" outer dia

Neodymium disc magnets, N35 strength, 12mm dia x 2mm high

Invisible sewing thread

Painter's tape

Craft Glue Dots, 1/2" diameter, permanent

Craft glue (Aleene's Tacky Glue or Elmer's Glue-All)

Fabric glue (Fabri-Tac preferred to prevent foam board from warping)

Pencil, ruler, utility knife, cutting mat, screwdriver, foam brush

1 cup uncooked rice, zipper plastic sandwich bag

Spray paint in yellow (optional)

Adhesive felt (optional)

FOAM BOARD CUT LIST

Draw pieces on foam board, label them with alpha character in parentheses, then cut with utility knife and ruler. For clean cuts, be sure to have a sharp blade in the knife. Protect your work surface with 2 layers of scrap cardboard or a cutting mat. If you would like to watch a video demo for cutting foam board, many are available on YouTube.

SIZE	QTY	PART	
6" x 6"	1	Back	(A)
4 13/16" x 6"	2	Sides	(B)
5" x 6"	1	Top	(C)
1 1/8" x 6"	1	Upper Front	(D)
1" x 6"	1	Lower Front	(E)
1" x 4 1/2"	4	Shelf Supports	(F)
1 5/8" x 5 5/8"	1	Door Stop	(G)
7/8" x 5 5/8"	1	Spacer	(H)
4 13/16" x 5 5/8"	1	Shelf	(J)
5 3/16" x 6"	1	Base	(K)
4" x 6"	1	Door	(L)

OVEN FRAME ASSEMBLY

Use painter's tape or craft glue for the frame assembly.

1. Tape or glue Sides (**B**) to Back (**A**). Tape or glue Top (**C**) on sides and back. See illustration below.

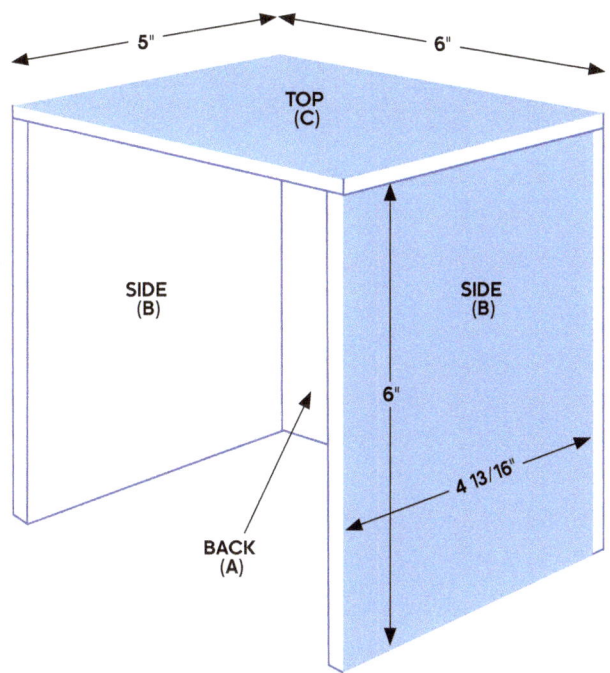

2. Tape or glue Upper Front (**D**) and Lower Front (**E**) as shown in illustration below.

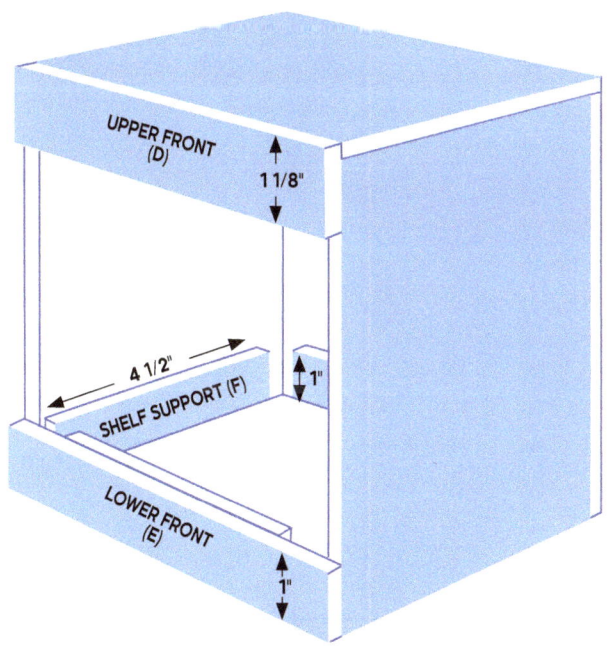

3. Glue Shelf Supports (**F**) to interior, one per side, aligned with bottom edge of oven and centered left-to-right. See illustration above.

4. Glue Spacer (**H**) atop Door Stop (**G**) with 2 long sides aligned. See illustration below.

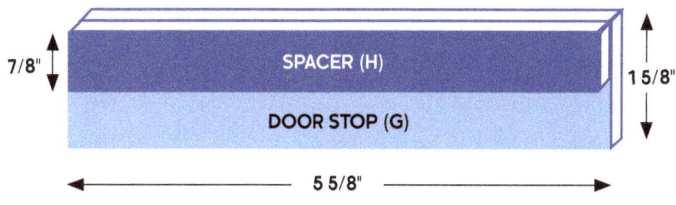

5. Glue Spacer (**H**) against back of Upper Front (**D**).

6. Tape or glue Base (**K**) to bottom of oven.

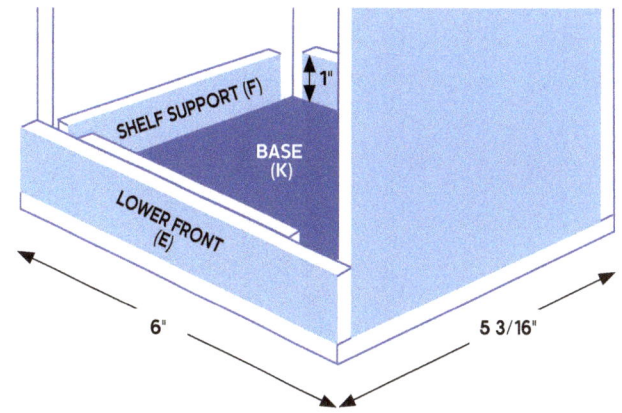

7. For base **weight**, seal uncooked rice in zipper sandwich bag. Place weight on base.

8. Check fit of Shelf (**J**) by setting it on shelf supports and make sure front edge lays **only on front shelf support**. The shelf must not overlap onto edge of Lower Front (**E**) or the oven door won't close properly. Trim shelf if needed. Once you have a good fit, apply craft glue along top edge of shelf supports and attach shelf.

9. Check fit of door by setting it in place. There should be a small gap (1/16"-1/8") between top of door and Upper Front (**D**). Trim door if needed. A fabric seal will close gap.

Set door aside. It will be attached later.

Now it's time to crochet!

GENERAL DIRECTIONS

Refer to the photos below for fabric dimensions as you work. **Your crocheted pieces must match these sizes to fit the oven frame.** Adjust your tension, hook size or chain length if needed.

DOOR

With green yarn, ch 27.

Rows 1-21: ch 1, turn, sc in each st across (27 sts). Fasten off.

UPPER FRONT

With pink yarn, ch 27.

Rows 1-5: ch 1, turn, sc in each st across (27 sts). Fasten off.

LOWER FRONT

With purple yarn, ch 27.

Rows 1-5: ch 1, turn, sc in each st across (27 sts). Fasten off.

TOP & SIDES

With light gray yarn, ch 24.

Rows 1-90: ch 1, turn, sc in each st across (24 sts). Fasten off.

BACK

With green yarn, ch 27.

Rows 1-34: ch 1, turn, sc in each st across (27 sts). Fasten off.

WINDOW

With charcoal yarn, ch 17.

Rows 1-8: ch 1, turn, sc in each st across (17 sts). Fasten off.

BURNERS (MAKE 4)

With charcoal yarn, make a magic ring, ch 1.

Rnd 1: 6 sc in ring, pull ring closed tight (6 sts).

Rnd 2: 2 sc in each st around. Place marker for beginning of rnd and move marker up as each rnd is completed (12 sts).

Rnd 3: *sc in next st, 2 sc in next st* 6 times (18 sts).

Rnd 4: *sc in next 2 sts, 2 sc in next st* 6 times (24 sts).

Rnd 5: *sc in next 3 sts, 2 sc in next st* 6 times (30 sts).

Sl st in next st. Fasten off. Weave in ends.

FABRIC DIMENSIONS

The crochet pieces pictured must match the measurements provided in these illustrations in order to fit the oven's frame.

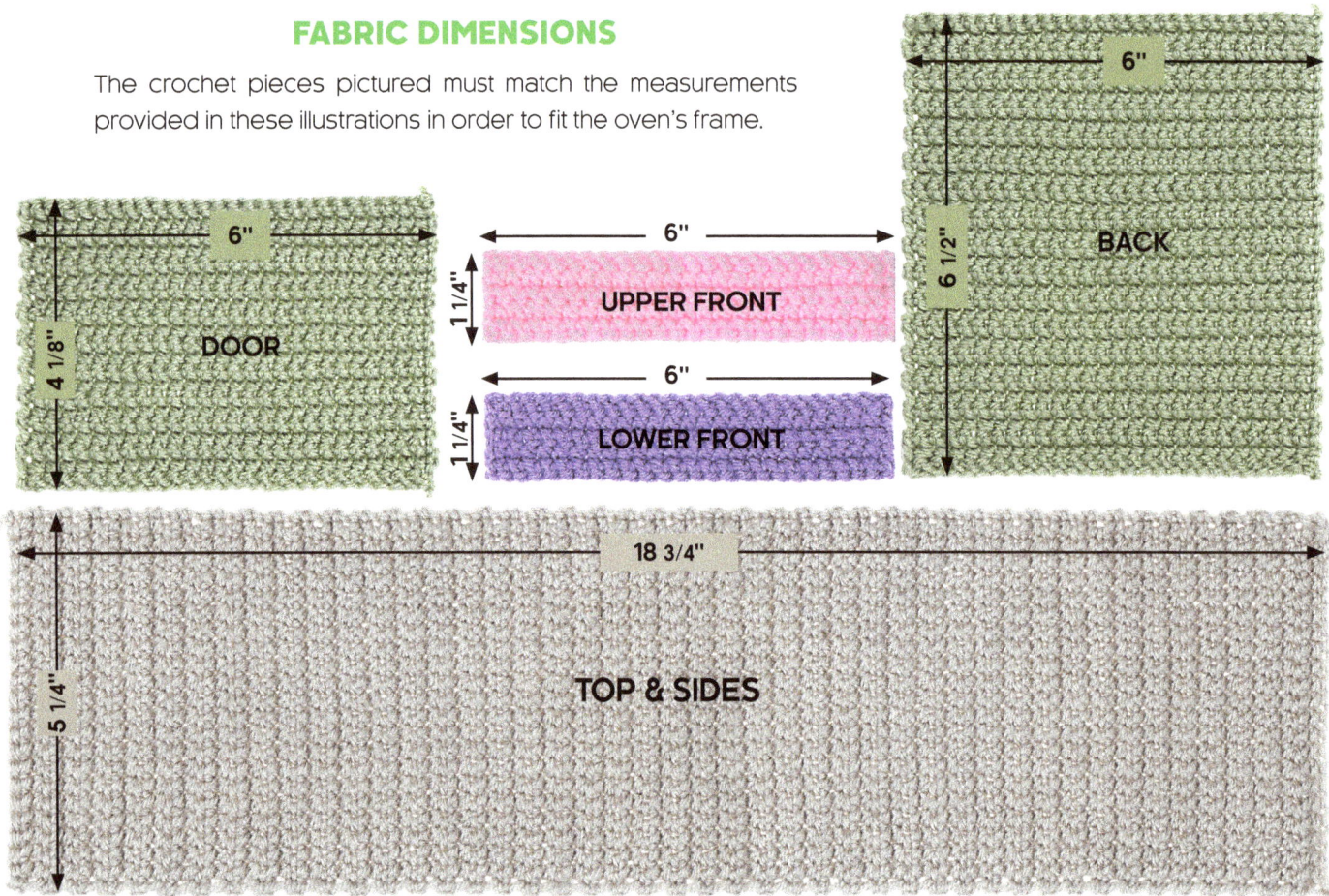

FINISHING

Sew buttons equally spaced to **pink** upper-front fabric.

With invisible sewing thread and whip stitch, sew **last row** of **green** door fabric to **last row** of **purple** lower-front fabric.

ATTACH FABRIC

Note: Use fabric glue when gluing crochet to foam board. Spread glue with foam brush if needed. Hide yarn tails between fabric and board.

Glue **pink** upper-front fabric to (D) with top edges aligned: the fabric will overhang lower edge of foam board ~1/8". This will create door seal. Glue **green** back fabric to (A). Glue **light gray** top/sides fabric around (B) and (C). Let dry.

ADD THE DOOR

Paint cabinet pull yellow if desired.

Final Fitting: Your yarn weight and size of overhang along Upper Front (D) may have affected the fit of your door so let's test it again. Set door in place and be sure it fits into the space between Upper Front (D) and Lower Front (E) with room to open and close smoothly. Trim door if needed.

Retrieve door fabric — the green and purple pieces that you sewed together. Leave the **purple** lower-front fabric hanging free and glue the **green** door fabric to Door (L) leaving ~1/16"-1/8" overhanging top edge of foam board to create door seal. Let dry.

Mark position for screw holes of cabinet pull so they are 3/4" below top of Door (L) and centered left-to-right. Poke holes thru **foam board and fabric** with a Phillips screwdriver at locations marked for screw holes. Put fender washers on screws and push screws thru holes at door back until they emerge at door front. Place cabinet pull atop screws and tighten with screwdriver.

Lay door in position and glue **purple** lower-front fabric to Lower Front (E).

MAKE LATCH

With **glue dots**, attach a magnet at each side of Door Stop (G). Note: Do not touch glue dots with your fingers. Press magnet onto dot, pull both from liner and stick firmly in place.

With **glue dots**, attach flat washers to back of Door (L) opposite magnets.

Note: The oven latch should hold the door closed gently and enable the door to be opened without pulling the whole oven toward you. Two magnets provided a good latch on my oven. If your 2 magnets are too strong, you can decrease their pull by cutting 2 circles of adhesive felt (use a spare magnet for a pattern) and sticking them on your oven's magnets. If your 2 magnets are too weak, a 3rd magnet can be added at center of Door Stop (G) with a washer opposite. Magnets can also be stacked to increase their strength.

ATTACH DETAILS

Glue **burners** to top of oven.

Glue **window** to front of door.

Oven Top

Baking Sheet

This pattern uses a mixture of ch, sc, hdc and sl st. The base of the Baking Sheet is worked in rows followed by a rim worked in rounds. Cardboard makes the sheet stiff.

SUPPLIES

G6/4mm crochet hook

Small amount of Worsted weight yarn in gray

Small piece of felt

Small piece of thin cardboard (e.g. cereal box)

Glue (for fabric, see page 11)

SIZE: 4" x 5"

Ch 18.

Rows 1-10: ch 1, turn, hdc in each st across (18 sts).

Now work in rounds.

Rnd 11: sc in each st around perimeter making 3 sts in same st at corners.

Rnd 12: working in **back loops only**, sc in each st around.

Rnd 13: resuming work in **both loops**, sl st in each st around.

Fasten off. Weave in ends.

FINISHING

Cut cardboard in a 3" x 4" rectangle with rounded corners.

Cut felt in a 3 1/2" x 4 1/2" rectangle with rounded corners.

Glue cardboard to felt, centered.

Glue cardboard/felt assembly to bottom of baking sheet, centered, with wrong sides facing.

Mixing Spoon

The mixing spoon is worked in 1 piece starting at the handle. A pipe cleaner provides stuffing and structure.

SUPPLIES

E4/3.5mm crochet hook

Small amount of DK, Light Worsted yarn

Pipe cleaner

Make a magic ring, ch 1.

Rnd 1: 6 sc in ring, pull ring closed tight (6 sts).

Rnds 2-16: for handle, sc in each st around. Place marker for beginning of rnd and move marker up as each rnd is completed (6 sts).

Rnd 17: for bowl, 2 sc in each st around (12 sts).

Rnd 18: sc in each st around.

Rnd 19: *sc in next 4 sts, 2 sc in next 2 sts* 2 times (16 sts).

Rnds 20-21: sc in each st around.

Rnd 22: *sc in next 4 sts, sc2tog twice* 2 times (12 sts).

Rnd 23: sc in each st around.

Frame: make frame following instructions below and slide into place.

Rnd 24: sc2tog 6 times (6 sts).

Fasten off. Thread ending tail onto needle, insert needle thru front loop of each stitch around opening and pull tight to close hole. Hide end inside.

FRAME

Hold narrow section of crochet hook against middle of pipe cleaner and bend pipe cleaner around hook to make a tiny U-shape. Lay pipe cleaner on spoon and bend into shape of spoon, twisting the area for handle. Twist ends together to connect the frame.

Tiny U-shape is here.

Lifting Spatula

The lifting spatula is worked in one piece starting with the blade. A pipe cleaner stuffs the handle and adds structure.

SUPPLIES

E4/3.5mm crochet hook

Small amount of DK, Light Worsted yarn in blue

Small amount of Worsted weight yarn in light gray

Pipe cleaner

With blue yarn, loosely ch 14, join with sl st to 1st ch to make a ring using care not to twist the chain.

Rnds 1-8: for blade, sc in each st around. Place marker for beginning of rnd and move marker up as each rnd is completed (14 sts).

Rnd 9: *sc in next 5 sts, sc2tog* twice (12 sts).

Rnd 10: *sc in next 4 sts, sc2tog* twice (10 sts).

Rnd 11: *sc in next 3 sts, sc2tog* twice (8 sts).

Rnds 12-27: for handle, sc in each st around.

Fasten off. Thread ending tail onto needle, insert needle thru front loop of each stitch of Rnd 27 and pull tight to close hole. Hide end inside.

Frame: make frame following instructions for Mixing Spoon. Slide frame thru open end of blade into spatula. Sew blade closed.

FINISHING

Mock slots: use light gray yarn to embroider 3 long sts on each side of blade as shown in photo.

Shaping: bend slightly where handle meets blade.

Frosting Spatula

The frosting spatula is worked in 2 pieces. The final assembly is done with glue which adds stiffness to the handle. I used Elmer's Glue-All.

SUPPLIES

E4/3.5mm crochet hook

Small amount of DK, Light Worsted yarn in off-white & purple

Glue (for crafts, see page 11)

Note: A chain 1 at the beginning of a row is for turning your work and does not count as a stitch.

PADDLE

With off-white yarn, make a magic ring, ch 1.

Rnd 1: 6 sc in ring, pull ring closed tight (6 sts).

Rnd 2: *3 sc in next st, 2 sc in next st, sc in next st* twice (12 sts).

Rnd 3: *2 sc in next st, sc in next 5 sts* twice (14 sts).

Rnds 4-9: sc in each st around.

Sl st in next st. Fasten off.

HANDLE

With purple yarn, loosely ch 30.

Rows 1-2: ch 1, turn, sc in each st across (30 sts).

Fasten off.

FINISHING

Fold handle in half widthwise, right sides facing, and glue layers together. Let dry.

Trim yarn tails to 1/2". Flatten paddle, insert handle and squirt in some glue. Finger-press to merge the layers. This will connect the layers of the paddle, stiffen it, and attach the handle.

Mixing Bowl

The Mixing Bowl is made in 2 layers that are connected at the top. For the best fit, use the same yarn brand for both layers.

SUPPLIES

G6/4mm crochet hook

Small amount of Worsted weight yarn in green and turquoise

OUTER BOWL

With green yarn, make a magic ring, ch 1.

Rnd 1: 6 sc in ring, pull ring closed tight (6 sts).

Rnd 2: 2 sc in each st around. Place marker for beginning of rnd and move marker up as each rnd is completed (12 sts).

Rnd 3: *sc in next st, 2 sc in next st* 6 times (18 sts).

Rnd 4: *sc in next 2 sts, 2 sc in next st* 6 times (24 sts).

Rnd 5: *sc in next 3 sts, 2 sc in next st* 6 times (30 sts).

Rnds 6-7: sc in each st around.

Rnd 8: *sc in next 4 sts, 2 sc in next st* 6 times (36 sts).

Rnds 9-10: sc in each st around.

Sl st in next st. Fasten off.

INNER BOWL

With turquoise yarn, make a magic ring, ch 1.

Rnd 1: 6 sc in ring, pull ring closed tight (6 sts).

Rnd 2: 2 sc in each st around. Place marker for beginning of rnd and move marker up as each rnd is completed (12 sts).

Rnd 3: *sc in next st, 2 sc in next st* 6 times (18 sts).

Rnd 4: *sc in next 2 sts, 2 sc in next st* 6 times (24 sts).

Rnd 5: *sc in next 3 sts, 2 sc in next st* 6 times (30 sts).

Rnds 6-7: sc in each st around.

Rnd 8: *sc in next 4 sts, 2 sc in next st* 6 times (36 sts).

Sl st in next st. Do not fasten off.

Nest inner bowl inside outer bowl with wrong sides together.

Rnd 9: working thru both layers, sc in each st around.

Fasten off. Hide yarn tails between layers.

Tea Towel

SUPPLIES

F5/3.75mm crochet hook

Small amount of DK, Light Worsted yarn in blue and orange

Note: A chain 1 at the beginning of a row is for turning your work and does not count as a stitch.

With blue yarn, loosely ch 14.

Row 1: ch 1, turn, dc in each st across; change to orange yarn in last st (14 sts).

Rows 2-3: ch 1, turn, sc in each st across; change to blue yarn in last st of Row 3. Cut off orange with 4" tail.

Rows 4-13: ch 1, turn, dc in each st across; change to orange yarn in last st of Row 13.

Rows 14-15: ch 1, turn, sc in each st across; change to blue yarn in last st of Row 15. Cut off orange with 4" tail.

Row 16: ch 1, turn, dc in each st across.

Row 17: ch 1, turn, sc in each st across.

Fasten off. Weave in ends.

Potholder

SUPPLIES

F5/3.75mm crochet hook

Small amount of DK, Light Worsted yarn in blue and orange

Note: A chain 1 at the beginning of a row is for turning your work and does not count as a stitch.

With blue yarn, loosely ch 7.

Rows 1-7: ch 1, turn, sc in each st across; change to orange yarn in last st of Rnd 7 (7 sts).

Rnd 8: ch 1, do not turn, sc in each st around perimeter making 3 sts in same st at corners.

For loop: tightly ch 8, sl st in same st as where your ch started. Fasten off. Weave in ends.

73

Cookie the Cat

SIZE

4" tall, not including ears

SUPPLIES

G6/4mm crochet hook

Small amount of Worsted weight yarn in white, black & pink

2 black safety eyes, 7mm

Glue (for eyes, see page 11), optional

Polyester fiberfill stuffing

HEAD

With white yarn, make a magic ring, ch 1.

Rnd 1: 6 sc in ring, pull ring closed tight (6 sts).

Rnd 2: 2 sc in each st around. Place marker for beginning of rnd and move marker up as each rnd is completed (12 sts).

Rnd 3: *sc in next st, 2 sc in next st* 6 times (18 sts).

Rnd 4: *sc in next 2 sts, 2 sc in next st* 6 times (24 sts).

Rnd 5: *sc in next 3 sts, 2 sc in next st* 6 times (30 sts).

Rnds 6-9: sc in each st around.

Work on face. Next the eyes are attached. (If preferred, these can be attached with glue after final assembly.)

- **Eyes:** Attach between Rnds 7-8 with an interspace of 6 sts.
- **Nose:** with pink yarn, embroider 1 or 2 small horizontal sts in groove below eyes.

Rnd 10: *sc in next 3 sts, sc2tog* 6 times (24 sts).

Rnd 11: *sc in next 2 sts, sc2tog* 6 times (18 sts).

Rnd 12: *sc in next 4 sts, sc2tog* 3 times (15 sts).

Sl st in next st. Fasten off.

Stuff head.

BODY

With white yarn, make a magic ring, ch 1.

Rnd 1: 6 sc in ring, pull ring closed tight (6 sts).

Rnd 2: 2 sc in each st around. Place marker for beginning of rnd and move marker up as each rnd is completed (12 sts).

Rnd 3: *sc in next st, 2 sc in next st* 6 times (18 sts).

Rnd 4: *sc in next 2 sts, 2 sc in next st* 6 times (24 sts).

Rnds 5-7: sc in each st around.

Rnd 8: *sc in next 2 sts, sc2tog* 6 times (18 sts).

Rnds 9-10: sc in each st around.

Rnd 11: *sc in next 4 sts, sc2tog* 3 times (15 sts).

Rnd 12: sc in each st around.

Sl st in next st. Fasten off.

Stuff body.

EARS (MAKE 2)

The ears are worked around a foundation chain.

Note: A chain 1 at the beginning of a rnd is for turning your work and does not count as a stitch.

EAR FRONT

With pink yarn, loosely ch 3.

Rnd 1: starting in 2nd ch from hook, sc in next ch, 3 sc in last ch, sc in next ch (5 sts). Fasten off.

EAR BACK

With black yarn, loosely ch 3.

Rnd 1: starting in 2nd ch from hook, sc in next ch, 3 sc in last ch, sc in next ch (5 sts).

Rnd 2: ch 1, turn, place ear front against ear back with wrong sides facing and sts aligned. Working thru both layers, sc in next 2 sts, 3 sc in next st, sc in next 2 sts (7 sts).

Rnd 3: ch 1, turn, sc in next 3 sts, 3 sc in next st, sc in next 3 sts (9 sts). Fasten off.

Sew first 3 tails into space between layers of ear to hide them, cut off excess.

Pinch tip of ear into a point.

ARMS (MAKE 2)

With white yarn, make a magic ring, ch 1.

Rnd 1: 6 sc in ring, pull ring closed tight (6 sts).

Rnd 2: *sc in next st, 2 sc in next st* 3 times. Place marker for beginning of rnd and move marker up as each rnd is completed (9 sts).

Rnds 3-4: sc in each st around.

Rnd 5: *sc in next st, sc2tog* 3 times; change to black yarn in last st (6 sts)

Rnds 6-10: sc in each st around.

Sl st in next st. Fasten off. Stuff paw only; do not stuff arm.

To make 2nd arm, work all rnds in white.

LEGS (MAKE 2)

With white yarn, make a magic ring, ch 1.

Rnd 1: 6 sc in ring, pull ring closed tight (6 sts).

Rnd 2: 2 sc in each st around. Place marker for beginning of rnd and move marker up as each rnd is completed (12 sts).

Rnd 3: sc in each st around; change to black yarn in last st.

Rnds 4-5: sc in each st around.

Rnd 6: *sc in next 2 sts, sc2tog* 3 times (9 sts).

Rnd 7: sc in each st around.

Sl st in next st. Fasten off. Stuff leg.

To make 2nd leg, work all rnds in white.

TAIL

With black yarn, make a magic ring, ch 1.

Rnd 1: 6 sc in ring, pull ring closed tight (6 sts).

Rnds 2-?: sc in each st around until tail is about 2 1/2" long.

Sl st in next st. Fasten off.

FINISHING

Sew **head** to body.

Sew **ears** with rims cupped on head: place inner edges on groove between Rnds 1-2.

Set body on a flat surface and pin **legs** to front as pictured so that cat will sit nicely. Sew legs in place.

Pin **tail** to back so that sitting cat won't topple backwards. Sew tail in place.

Sew **arms** to sides of body as pictured.

Weave in ends.

Donut the Dog

Donut's ears get a bit of bling with shimmery sprinkles! A black animal eye can be substituted for the triangle nose if desired.

SIZE

4" tall

SUPPLIES

G6/4mm crochet hook

Small amount of Worsted weight yarn in light pink, dark pink and black

2 black safety eyes, 7mm

Black triangle animal nose, 7mm

Bugle beads in assorted colors, 6mm

Glue (for beads, see page 11)

Polyester fiberfill stuffing

EYE PATCH

With dark pink yarn, make a magic ring, ch 1.

Rnd 1: 6 sc in ring, pull ring closed almost tight (6 sts).

Sl st in next st. Fasten off.

HEAD

With light pink yarn, make a magic ring, ch 1.

Rnd 1: 6 sc in ring, pull ring closed almost tight (6 sts).

Rnd 2: 2 sc in each st around. Place marker for beginning of rnd and move marker up as each rnd is completed (12 sts).

Rnds 3-4: sc in each st around.

Rnd 5: *sc in next st, 2 sc in next st* 6 times (18 sts).

Rnd 6: *sc in next 2 sts, 2 sc in next st* 6 times (24 sts).

Rnd 7: *sc in next 3 sts, 2 sc in next st* 6 times (30 sts).

Rnds 8-11: sc in each st around.

Work on face. Next the nose and eyes are attached. (If preferred, these features can be attached with glue after final assembly.)

- **Nose:** with black yarn, embroider a stitch from center of Rnd 1 to groove between Rnds 2-3 as pictured. Attach nose at center of Rnd 1.

- **Eyes:** with eye patch <u>wrong side up</u>, insert post of 1 eye thru center and attach to head between Rnds 6-7 as shown in photo. Attach 2nd eye with an interspace of 5-6 sts. To secure eye patch, sew around rim with thread.

Rnd 12: *sc in next 3 sts, sc2tog* 6 times (24 sts).

Rnd 13: *sc in next 2 sts, sc2tog* 6 times (18 sts).

Rnd 14: *sc in next 4 sts, sc2tog* 3 times (15 sts).

Start to stuff head and continue stuffing after each rnd.

Rnd 15: *sc in next 3 sts, sc2tog* 3 times (12 sts).

Rnd 16: sc2tog 6 times (6 sts).

Fasten off.

Finish adding stuffing. To close hole, thread tail in yarn needle, insert needle thru front loop of each st around opening and pull tight. Weave in end. Squeeze head into shape.

BODY

With light pink yarn, make a magic ring, ch 1.

Rnd 1: 6 sc in ring, pull ring closed tight (6 sts).

Rnd 2: 2 sc in each st around. Place marker for beginning of rnd and move marker up as each rnd is completed (12 sts).

Rnd 3: *sc in next st, 2 sc in next st* 6 times (18 sts).

Rnd 4: *sc in next 2 sts, 2 sc in next st* 6 times (24 sts).

Rnds 5-7: sc in each st around.

Rnd 8: *sc in next 2 sts, sc2tog* 6 times (18 sts).

Rnds 9-10: sc in each st around.

Rnd 11: *sc in next 4 sts, sc2tog* 3 times (15 sts).

Rnd 12: sc in each st around.

Sl st in next st. Fasten off.

Stuff body.

EARS (MAKE 2)

With dark pink yarn, ch 4.

Note: A chain 1 at the beginning of a row is for turning your work and does not count as a stitch.

Rows 1-6: ch 1, turn, sc in each st across (4 sts).

The remaining rows <u>do not</u> have a turning chain.

Row 7: turn, skip first st, sc in each remaining st across (3 sts).

Row 8: turn, skip first st, sc in each remaining st across (2 sts).

Row 9: turn, skip first st, sc in next st (1 st).

Rnd 10: sc around perimeter making 3 sts in same st at top corners (see blue dots).

Sl st in next st. Fasten off.

Glue bugle beads randomly to right side.

ARMS (MAKE 2)

With light pink yarn, make a magic ring, ch 1.

Rnd 1: 6 sc in ring, pull ring closed tight (6 sts).

Rnd 2: *sc in next st, 2 sc in next st* 3 times. Place marker for beginning of rnd and move marker up as each rnd is completed (9 sts).

Rnds 3-4: sc in each st around.

Rnd 5: *sc in next st, sc2tog* 3 times (6 sts)

Rnds 6-10: sc in each st around.

Sl st in next st. Fasten off. Stuff paw only; do not stuff arm.

LEGS (MAKE 2)

With dark pink yarn, make a magic ring, ch 1.

Rnd 1: 6 sc in ring, pull ring closed tight (6 sts).

Rnd 2: 2 sc in each st around; join with sl st in first st and change to light pink yarn in the sl st. Place marker for beginning of rnd and move marker up as each rnd is completed (12 sts).

Rnds 3-5: sc in each st around.

Rnd 6: *sc in next 2 sts, sc2tog* 3 times (9 sts).

Rnd 7: sc in each st around.

Sl st in next st. Fasten off.

Stuff leg.

TAIL

With dark pink yarn, make a magic ring, ch 1.

Rnd 1: 4 sc in ring, pull ring closed tight (4 sts).

Rnd 2: *sc in next st, 2 sc in next st* 2 times (6 sts).

Rnds 3-?: sc in each st around until tail is about 2" long.

Sl st in next st. Fasten off.

FINISHING

Sew **head** to body as shown in picture below.

Place front corners of **ears** on Rnd 10 of head and angle the back corners as shown in picture. Sew in place.

Set body on a flat surface and pin **legs** to front as pictured so that dog will sit nicely. Sew legs in place.

Pin **tail** to back so that sitting dog won't topple backwards. Sew tail in place.

Sew **arms** to sides of body as pictured.

Weave in ends.

Biscuit the Bear

A black animal eye can be substituted for the triangle animal nose if desired.

SIZE

4" tall, not including ears

SUPPLIES

G6/4mm crochet hook

Small amount of Worsted weight yarn in blue, white & black

2 black safety eyes, 7mm

Black triangle animal nose, 7mm

Glue (for eyes/nose, see page 11), optional

Polyester fiberfill stuffing

HEAD

With white yarn, make a magic ring, ch 1.

Rnd 1: 6 sc in ring, pull ring closed almost tight (6 sts).

Rnd 2: 2 sc in each st around. Place marker for beginning of rnd and move marker up as each rnd is completed (12 sts).

Rnds 3-4: sc in each st around; change to blue yarn in last st of Rnd 4.

Rnd 5: *sc in next st, 2 sc in next st* 6 times (18 sts).

Rnd 6: *sc in next 2 sts, 2 sc in next st* 6 times (24 sts).

Rnd 7: *sc in next 3 sts, 2 sc in next st* 6 times (30 sts).

Rnds 8-11: sc in each st around.

Work on face. Next the nose and eyes are attached. (If preferred, these features can be attached with glue after final assembly.)

- **Nose:** with black yarn, embroider a stitch from center of Rnd 1 to groove between Rnds 2-3 as pictured. Attach nose at center of Rnd 1.

- **Eyes:** attach to head between Rnds 6-7 with an interspace of 5-6 sts.

Rnd 12: *sc in next 3 sts, sc2tog* 6 times (24 sts).

Rnd 13: *sc in next 2 sts, sc2tog* 6 times (18 sts).

Rnd 14: *sc in next 4 sts, sc2tog* 3 times (15 sts).

Start to stuff head and continue stuffing after each rnd.

Rnd 15: *sc in next 3 sts, sc2tog* 3 times (12 sts).

Rnd 16: sc2tog 6 times (6 sts).

Fasten off.

Finish adding stuffing. To close hole, thread tail in yarn needle, insert needle thru front loop of each st around opening and pull tight. Weave in end. Squeeze head into shape.

BODY

With blue yarn, make a magic ring, ch 1.

Rnd 1: 6 sc in ring, pull ring closed tight (6 sts).

Rnd 2: 2 sc in each st around. Place marker for beginning of rnd and move marker up as each rnd is completed (12 sts).

Rnd 3: *sc in next st, 2 sc in next st* 6 times (18 sts).

Rnd 4: *sc in next 2 sts, 2 sc in next st* 6 times (24 sts).

Rnds 5-7: sc in each st around.

Rnd 8: *sc in next 2 sts, sc2tog* 6 times (18 sts).

Rnds 9-10: sc in each st around.

Rnd 11: *sc in next 4 sts, sc2tog* 3 times (15 sts).

Rnd 12: sc in each st around.

Sl st in next st. Fasten off.

Stuff body.

EARS (MAKE 2)

With blue yarn, make a magic ring, ch 1.

Rnd 1: 5 sc in ring, pull ring closed tight (5 sts).

Rnd 2: 2 sc in each st around. Place marker for beginning of rnd and move marker up as each rnd is completed (10 sts).

Rnds 3-4: sc in each st around.

Fasten off.

ARMS (MAKE 2)

With blue yarn, make a magic ring, ch 1.

Rnd 1: 6 sc in ring, pull ring closed tight (6 sts).

Rnd 2: *sc in next st, 2 sc in next st* 3 times. Place marker for beginning of rnd and move marker up as each rnd is completed (9 sts).

Rnds 3-4: sc in each st around.

Rnd 5: *sc in next st, sc2tog* 3 times (6 sts)

Rnds 6-10: sc in each st around.

Sl st in next st. Fasten off. Stuff paw only; do not stuff arm.

LEGS (MAKE 2)

With blue yarn, make a magic ring, ch 1.

Rnd 1: 6 sc in ring, pull ring closed tight (6 sts).

Rnd 2: 2 sc in each st around. Place marker for beginning of rnd and move marker up as each rnd is completed (12 sts).

Rnds 3-5: sc in each st around.

Rnd 6: *sc in next 2 sts, sc2tog* 3 times (9 sts).

Rnd 7: sc in each st around.

Sl st in next st. Fasten off.

Stuff legs.

TAIL

With blue yarn, make a magic ring, ch 1.

Rnd 1: 4 sc in ring, pull ring closed tight (4 sts).

Rnd 2: 2 sc in each st around. Place marker for beginning of rnd and move marker up as each rnd is completed (8 sts).

Rnd 3: sc in each st around.

Sl st in next st. Fasten off.

FINISHING

Sew **head** to body as shown in pictures.

Flatten **ears** and sew to head on Rnds 10-11.

Set body on a flat surface and pin **legs** to front as pictured so that bear will sit nicely. Sew legs in place.

Pin **tail** to back so that sitting bear won't topple backwards. Sew tail in place, pushing in a bit of stuffing when a small gap remains.

Sew **arms** to sides of body as pictured.

Weave in ends.

Muffin the Mouse

SIZE

4" tall, not including ears

SUPPLIES

G6/4mm crochet hook

Small amount of Worsted weight yarn in gray and pink

2 black safety eyes, 7mm

Glue (for eyes, see page 11), optional

Polyester fiberfill stuffing

HEAD

With gray yarn, make a magic ring, ch 1.

Rnd 1: 6 sc in ring, pull ring closed tight (6 sts).

Rnd 2: *sc in next st, 2 sc in next st* 3 times. Place marker for beginning of rnd and move marker up as each rnd is completed (9 sts).

Rnd 3: *sc in next 2 sts, 2 sc in next st* 3 times (12 sts).

Rnd 4: *sc in next 2 sts, 2 sc in next st* 4 times (16 sts).

Rnd 5: *sc in next 3 sts, 2 sc in next st* 4 times (20 sts).

Rnd 6: *sc in next 4 sts, 2 sc in next st* 4 times (24 sts).

Rnd 7: sc in each st around.

Rnd 8: *sc in next 5 sts, 2 sc in next st* 4 times (28 sts).

Rnds 9-11: sc in each st around.

Rnd 12: *sc in next 5 sts, sc2tog* 4 times (24 sts).

Rnd 13: *sc in next 2 sts, sc2tog* 6 times (18 sts).

Work on face. Next the eyes are attached. (If preferred, these can be attached with glue after final assembly.)

- **Eyes:** attach to head between Rnds 5-6 with an interspace of 5 sts.

- **Nose:** use pink yarn to embroider straight sts fanning out from center of Rnd 1 and extending out to Rnd 2 as shown in picture.

Rnd 14: *sc in next st, sc2tog* 6 times (12 sts).

Start to stuff head.

Rnd 15: *sc in next st, sc2tog* 4 times (8 sts).

Fasten off. Finish adding stuffing.

To close hole, thread tail in yarn needle, insert needle thru front loop of each st around opening and pull tight. Weave in end. Squeeze head into shape.

BODY

With gray yarn, make a magic ring, ch 1.

Rnd 1: 6 sc in ring, pull ring closed tight (6 sts).

Rnd 2: 2 sc in each st around. Place marker for beginning of rnd and move marker up as each rnd is completed (12 sts).

Rnd 3: *sc in next st, 2 sc in next st* 6 times (18 sts).

Rnd 4: *sc in next 2 sts, 2 sc in next st* 6 times (24 sts).

Rnds 5-7: sc in each st around.

Rnd 8: *sc in next 2 sts, sc2tog* 6 times (18 sts).

Rnds 9-10: sc in each st around.

Rnd 11: *sc in next 4 sts, sc2tog* 3 times (15 sts).

Rnd 12: sc in each st around.

Sl st in next st. Fasten off.

Stuff body.

EARS (MAKE 2)

Note: A chain 1 at the beginning of a rnd is for turning your work and does not count as a stitch.

EAR FRONT

With pink yarn, make a magic ring, ch 1.

Rnd 1: 6 sc in ring, pull ring closed tight (6 sts).

Rnd 2: sc in next st, 2 sc in next 4 sts, sc in next st (10 sts). Fasten off.

EAR BACK

With gray yarn, make a magic ring, ch 1.

Rnd 1: 6 sc in ring, pull ring closed tight (6 sts).

Rnd 2: sc in next st, 2 sc in next 4 sts, sc in next st (10 sts).

Rnd 3: ch 1, turn, place ear front on top of ear back with wrong sides facing and sts aligned. Working thru both layers, *sc in next st, 2 sc in next st* 5 times (15 sts).

Fasten off.

Sew first 3 tails into space between layers of ear to hide them, cut off excess. To shape the ear, thread ending tail in yarn needle, sew thru opposite corner (see arrow in photo below), pull tight and secure with a knot.

ARMS (MAKE 2)

With gray yarn, make a magic ring, ch 1.

Rnd 1: 6 sc in ring, pull ring closed tight (6 sts).

Rnd 2: *sc in next st, 2 sc in next st* 3 times. Place marker for beginning of rnd and move marker up as each rnd is completed (9 sts).

Rnds 3-4: sc in each st around.

Rnd 5: *sc in next st, sc2tog* 3 times (6 sts)

Rnds 6-10: sc in each st around.

Sl st in next st. Fasten off. Stuff hand only; do not stuff arm.

LEGS (MAKE 2)

With gray yarn, make a magic ring, ch 1.

Rnd 1: 6 sc in ring, pull ring closed tight (6 sts).

Rnd 2: 2 sc in each st around. Place marker for beginning of rnd and move marker up as each rnd is completed (12 sts).

Rnds 3-5: sc in each st around.

Rnd 6: *sc in next 2 sts, sc2tog* 3 times (9 sts).

Rnd 7: sc in each st around.

Sl st in next st. Fasten off.

Stuff legs.

TAIL

With gray yarn, ch 21.

Row 1: sl st in 2nd ch from hook and in each remaining ch across (20 sts).

Fasten off.

FINISHING

Sew **head** to body as shown in pictures.

Sew **ears** on Rnd 9 of head as shown in pictures.

Set body on a flat surface and pin **legs** to front as pictured so that mouse will sit nicely. Sew legs in place.

Sew **arms** to sides of body as pictured.

Sew **tail** to back of body.

Weave in ends.

Cupcake Sleeping Bag

Charlotte will have sweet dreams in this cozy bed! The frosting is stuffed lightly to make a pillow. By working the cupcake paper in back loops only, a ribbed effect is created.

SUPPLIES

H8/5mm crochet hook

95 yds of Worsted weight yarn in pink

180 yds of Worsted weight yarn in turquoise

Small amount of Worsted weight yarn in white, red, yellow, purple and green

Polyester fiberfill stuffing

Invisible sewing thread

Note: A chain 1 at the beginning of a row is for turning your work and does not count as a stitch.

FROSTING

With pink yarn, make a magic ring, ch 1.

Rnd 1: 10 hdc in ring, pull ring closed tight (10 sts).

Rnd 2: 2 hdc in each st around. Place marker for beginning of rnd and move marker up as each rnd is completed (20 sts).

Rnd 3: hdc in each st around.

Rnd 4: 2 hdc in each st around (40 sts).

Rnd 5: hdc in each st around.

Rnd 6: *hdc in next st, 2 hdc in next st* 20 times (60 sts).

Rnd 7: hdc in each st around.

Rnd 8: *hdc in next 2 sts, 2 hdc in next st* 20 times (80 sts).

Rnd 9: hdc in each st around.

Rnd 10: *hdc in next 3 sts, 2 hdc in next st* 20 times (100 sts).

Rnd 11: hdc in each st around.

Rnd 12: *hdc in next 4 sts, 2 hdc in next st* 20 times (120 sts).

Rnd 13: hdc in each st around.

Fold circle in half with wrong sides facing as shown in illustration below.

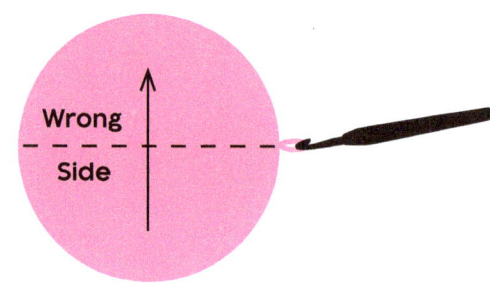

To connect the halves and create a pillow, ch 1, work stitch-by-stitch thru both layers with sl st. When you are halfway across, start stuffing lightly and continue stuffing lightly as you work.

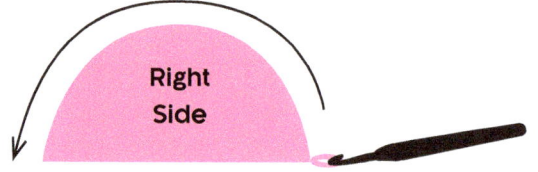

Fasten off. Hide end inside.

CUPCAKE PAPER

With turquoise yarn, ch 41 loosely.

Row 1: hdc in 2nd ch from hook and in each remaining ch across (40 sts).

Rows 2-56?: ch 1, turn, working in **back loops only**, hdc in each st across (40 sts).

Note: The cupcake paper needs to be twice the width of the frosting's straight side. Check your size as you near the final rows and adjust if needed by adding or subtracting rows. Do not fasten off.

Connect your **foundation chain** and **final row** as follows: ch 1, sl st in each st across thru both layers to form a tube. When you reach the corner, ch 1, sl st in each st across lower edge thru both layers. This will close up the bottom. Fasten off. Hide end inside.

Using invisible thread, sew **back edge** of cupcake paper to frosting as shown in picture.

SCALLOPS

With white yarn, ch 41 loosely.

Row 1: sc in 2nd ch from hook and in each remaining ch across (40 sts).

Row 2: ch 1, turn, *sc in next st, hdc in next st, dc in next st, tr in next st, 3 tr in next st, tr in next st, dc in next st, hdc in next st, sc in next st, sl st in next st* 4 times (4 scallops).

Row 3: ch 1, turn, *sc in next st, hdc in next st, dc in next st, tr in next 2 sts, 3 tr in next st, tr in next 2 sts, dc in next st, hdc in next st, sc in next st, sl st in next st* 4 times.

Fasten off with extra long tail. Pin scallops to **front edge** of cupcake paper as shown in picture. Sew in place with yarn tail.

CHERRY

With red yarn, make a magic ring, ch 1.

Rnd 1: 6 sc in ring, pull ring closed tight (6 sts).

Rnd 2: 2 sc in each st around. Place marker for beginning of rnd and move marker up as each rnd is completed (12 sts).

Rnd 3: *sc in next st, 2 sc in next st* 6 times (18 sts).

Rnds 4-6: sc in each st around.

Rnd 7: *sc in next st, sc2tog* 6 times (12 sts).

Fasten off. Stuff the cherry. Thread ending tail onto needle, insert needle thru front loop of each stitch around opening and pull tight to close hole. Sew to top of frosting as shown in picture.

SPRINKLES (MAKE 5)

With assorted colors of yarn, ch 6 loosely.

Row 1: sc in 2nd ch from hook and in each remaining ch across (5 sts).

Fasten off. Knot tails together. Sew to frosting as shown in picture. Hide tails inside.

Sweet Dreams

Stitches

SLIP KNOT

This is used to make a starting loop on the crochet hook.

1. Make a loop about 5 inches from end of yarn. Insert hook in loop and hook onto supply yarn (yarn coming from ball) at A.

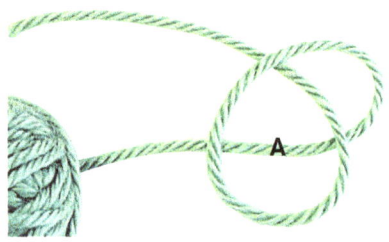

2. Pull yarn through loop.

3. Pull yarn ends to tighten loop around hook.

CHAIN (CH)

Start with a slip knot on hook.

1. Bring yarn **over** hook from back to front. Catch yarn with hook and pull it through the loop —

to look like this. One ch is done.

SLIP STITCH (SL ST)

1. Insert hook in stitch. Yarn over and pull through stitch and through loop on hook (A and B).

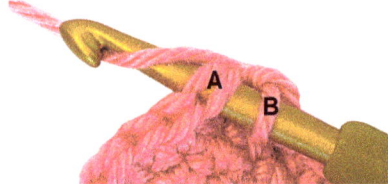

2. The sl st is done.

SINGLE CROCHET (SC)

This simple stitch is the primary stitch for amigurumi.

1. Insert hook in designated stitch. Note: Put hook under **both loops** that form v-shape at top of stitch unless otherwise instructed.

2. Yarn over and pull through the stitch (A).

You now have 2 loops on the hook:

3. Yarn over and pull through both loops on hook.

4. You now have 1 loop on hook and the sc stitch is done.

HALF DOUBLE CROCHET (HDC)

1. Yarn over and insert hook in designated stitch.

2. Yarn over and pull through the stitch (A).

You now have 3 loops on hook:

3. Yarn over and pull through all 3 loops on hook (A, B & C).

4. You now have 1 loop on hook and the hdc stitch is done.

DOUBLE CROCHET (DC)

1. Yarn over and insert hook in designated stitch.

2. Yarn over and pull through the stitch (A).

You now have 3 loops on hook:

3. Yarn over and pull through 1st 2 loops on hook (A and B).

You now have 2 loops on hook:

4. Yarn over and pull through both loops on hook.

5. You now have 1 loop on hook and the dc stitch is done.

TRIPLE OR TREBLE CROCHET (TR)

1. Yarn over **twice** and insert hook in stitch.

2. Yarn over and pull yarn through the stitch, bringing up a loop.

3. Yarn over again and pull yarn through **first 2 loops** on hook.

4. Yarn over again and pull yarn through **next 2 loops** on hook.

5. Yarn over again and pull yarn through **last 2 loops** on hook.

6. You now have 1 loop on hook and the tr stitch is done.

SINGLE CROCHET 2 TOGETHER DECREASE (SC2TOG)

This stitch is used to decrease 2 stitches into 1 stitch.

1. Insert hook in first stitch, yarn over and pull up a loop. You now have 2 loops on hook.

2. Insert hook in next stitch, yarn over and pull up a loop. You now have 3 loops on hook.

3. Yarn over and pull through all 3 loops on hook.

INVISIBLE DECREASE (INVDEC)

This is a very neat way to decrease 2 stitches into 1 stitch.

1. Insert hook in **front loop** of first st. DO NOT YARN OVER. You now have 2 loops on hook.

2. Insert hook in **front loop** of next st. You now have 3 loops on hook.

3. Yarn over and pull through first 2 loops on hook. You now have 2 loops on hook.

4. Yarn over and pull through both loops on hook.

SINGLE CROCHET 3 TOGETHER DECREASE (SC3TOG)

This stitch is used to decrease 3 stitches into 1 stitch.

1. Insert hook in first stitch, yarn over and pull up a loop. You now have 2 loops on hook.

2. Insert hook in next stitch, yarn over and pull up a loop. You now have 3 loops on hook.

3. Insert hook in next stitch, yarn over and pull up a loop. You now have 4 loops on hook.

4. Yarn over and pull through all 4 loops on hook.

85

Techniques

★ MAGIC RING

Most of my amigurumi begins with the magic ring. This is an adjustable loop that makes a neat center when crocheting in the round. If you're not familiar with it, you may want to watch a YouTube tutorial. It's not difficult — and well worth it.

An alternative to the magic ring, if desired, is to ch 2; then begin Rnd 1 by working the required number of sts as stated in the pattern into the 2nd ch from the hook. This method is perfectly acceptable but will leave a small hole in the middle of the first round (see photo below).

Magic Ring

Ch 2

Make the Magic Ring as follows:

1. Make a ring a few inches from end of yarn. Grasp ring between thumb and index finger where the join makes an X. Insert hook in ring, hook onto supply yarn at Y and pull up a loop —

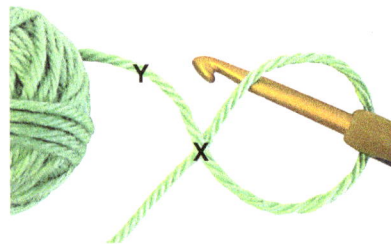

to look like this.

2. Chain 1 —

to look like this. This chain does not count as a stitch.

3. Insert hook into ring so you're crocheting over ring and yarn tail. Pull up a loop to begin your first single crochet —

and complete the single crochet.

4. Continue to crochet over ring and yarn tail for the specified number of single crochets for the 1st round.

5. Pull tail to close up ring. To begin the 2nd round, insert hook in 1st stitch of 1st round (see arrow).

BEGIN 2ND RND HERE

WORKING IN THE ROUND

Working in the round is crocheting in a continuous spiral. Lots of amigurumi is worked this way.

WORKING IN LOOPS

When a single crochet stitch is made, you will see 2 loops in a v-shape at the top of the stitch. To crochet the patterns in this book, insert your hook under **both loops** unless instructed otherwise. Crocheting in the "front loops only" or the "back loops only" is sometimes used for a different effect.

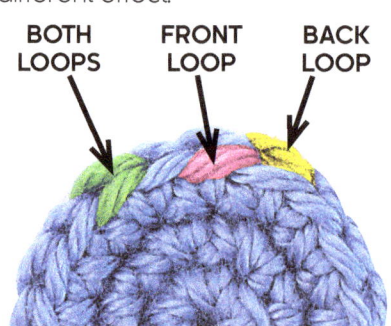
BOTH LOOPS   FRONT LOOP   BACK LOOP

CHANGING COLORS

To change color while single crocheting, work last stitch of old color to last yarn over, yarn over with new color and pull through both loops to complete the stitch.

ROTATING YOUR HOOK

When you wrap yarn over your hook, the front of the hook should be facing you. Then when it's time to pull the yarn through the loop on the hook, rotate the hook downward. It will slide easily through the loop instead of getting caught.

COUNTING ROUNDS

Periodically, it is good to count your rounds to ensure your place in a pattern. Fortunately, rounds are clearly defined and counting is easy. Each round makes a ridge. A groove separates the rounds. You need only to count the ridges. Take a look at the photo below to see that the circle has 5 rounds.

USING STITCH MARKERS

It can be tricky to keep track of your place when working in the round, so be sure to use a stitch marker. Place the stitch marker in the first stitch of a round — after completing the stitch. When you've crocheted all the way around, remove the stitch marker, make the next stitch, and replace the marker in the stitch just made. This will be the first stitch of the next round.

RUNNING STITCH MARKER

Stitch markers are essential in amigurumi to mark specific spots on your work. You can use one any time you feel it is necessary and sometimes the pattern will indicate that a marker is needed. A Running Stitch Marker is a scrap of yarn in a contrasting color that is woven back and forth between rounds. I especially like this type of marker for narrow cylinders such as arms and legs.

When you complete your first round, lay your "marker-yarn" over your work before starting the next round. Then, when you work the first stitch of the next round, the yarn will be trapped between the stitches. At the end of each successive round, fold the marker-yarn back over your work: if it's in the back, fold it to the front, if it's in the front, fold it to the back. This way the yarn is flipped back and forth — between the last stitch of each round and the first stitch of the next round. When you're done, simply pull the marker-yarn out.

FASTENING OFF

This is the way to finish a piece so that it won't unravel. When you're done crocheting, cut the yarn and leave a tail. Wrap the tail over your hook and pull it all the way through the last loop left on your hook. Pull the tail tight and it will make a knot.

SMOOTHING THE EDGE

When fastening off, the knot can make a small bump in the edge of your work so that, for example, a round shape will not look as round as it should. To make the edge smooth, thread the long tail in a yarn needle and insert the needle down thru the center "V" of the next stitch.

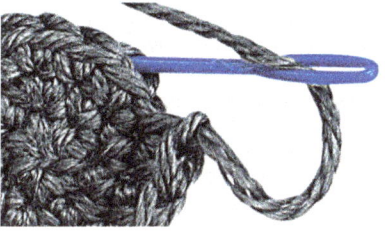

JOINING YARN

To join new yarn onto a crocheted item, such as to make a border, strap or sleeve, insert hook in desired stitch, make a loop and pull it through the stitch.

JOINING WITH SL ST

Start with a Slip Knot on hook. Insert hook in specified stitch. Yarn over and pull through the stitch and the loop on the hook.

JOINING WITH SC

Put yarn on hook with a Slip Knot. Insert hook in indicated stitch. Complete sc as shown in Single Crochet tutorial, page 84, steps 2-4

ASSEMBLING

The assembly stage of amigurumi is an exciting time. This is when various pieces are sewn together and the project blossoms in cuteness! Thread a yarn needle with the tail of your auxiliary piece (arm, leg, etc.) and use a whip stitch or running stitch to sew it in place. You may want to pin your pieces in place beforehand to be sure the position looks good. A sewing needle and thread can also be used to sew your parts together. In some cases, this will make the stitches less visible.

WEAVING IN ENDS

The assembly of every pattern includes the instruction to weave in the ends. This is the way to hide and secure all of your straggly yarn tails. Follow this "Rule of 3": (1) Thread yarn tail into a yarn needle, skim thru back of sts on wrong side of work for a short distance; (2) turn and go in opposite direction thru different sts; (3) turn and go in original direction to lock the yarn in place. Trim end close. When you turn to the right side, you should not see the woven ends. They should be tucked into the middle of your crocheted fabric.

FRENCH KNOT

Bring needle up from wrong side at A. Place needle close to fabric and wrap yarn around needle 2 or 3 times. Push needle down at a point near A.

RUNNING STITCH

The Running Stitch is formed by a detached series of Straight Stitches. Make it by running the needle up and down the fabric at a regular distance. Come up at A, down at B, up at C, down at D, up at E, down at F, etc.

A B   C D   E F

ADDING WIRE

Optional armatures, or wire frameworks, can make amigurumi more dynamic by enabling a character to hold a pose. It can be placed in the arms, legs or both.

PARTIAL ARMATURE

If your doll is made for display, this will make your doll more like an action figure than a cuddly stuffie. Use a heavy wire of 16 to 19 gauge. Begin when the doll's head/body are stuffed and connected and all parts are made.

For the **arms**, stuff hands only. The arms won't need stuffed. Lay doll down with arms outstretched in position and cut a piece of wire to that length plus a bit extra (~1/2" to 1").

1. Bend one end into a small loop with needle-nose pliers and insert into first arm thru to hand.

2. Insert exposed end of wire into body where the arm will be placed.

3. Push wire all the way thru body to opposite side where you will sew the other arm.

4. Bend exposed tip of wire into a small loop and insert into 2nd arm.

5. Sew both arms to body around wire core.

For yarn-jointed **legs**, prepare a piece of wire the length of each leg with a small loop at each end. Insert wire in leg and stuff around it using long craft tweezers. Finish assembly according to pattern instructions. Note: When pushing needle thru top of leg for yarn-jointing (see page 16, Fig. X) be sure needle goes thru loop at top of wire.

BOW

Use this 2-inch bow to embellish the Chef Dress for a pretty variation. With 7/8" satin ribbon, cut a 12" piece and make a loop as shown below. Tip: wrap ribbon around 3 fingers to make the loop. Pin in place.

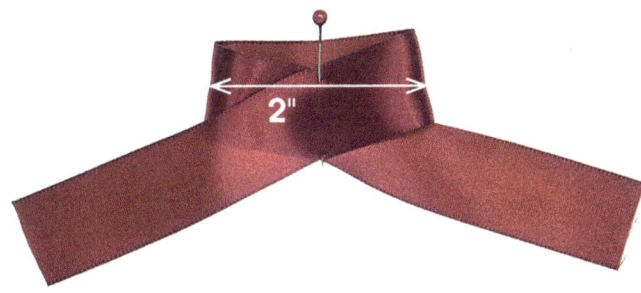

Sew thru all layers with running stitch along the center.

Pull thread tight to gather. Wrap thread around center 3 times and fasten with a knot. Trim ends at an angle. To prevent fraying, sweep edges along a flame to melt the fibers or apply clear nail polish.

For **center piece**, cut a 2" piece of ribbon and fold it lengthwise in thirds. Wrap strip around middle of bow, cinch tightly, cut off excess & sew in place with whip stitch.

Resources

YARN

Amazon
amazon.com

Herrschners
herrschners.com

Lovecrafts
lovecrafts.com

Michaels
michaels.com

NOTIONS

Amazon
amazon.com

Joann Fabric and Craft Stores
joann.com

SAFETY EYES

Amazon
amazon.com

Etsy
etsy.com

BEADS

Amazon
amazon.com

Etsy
etsy.com

Michaels
michaels.com

CAKE PLATE HARDWARE

Amazon
amazon.com

Ebay
ebay.com

Etsy
etsy.com

VIDEO TUTORIALS

YouTube
youtube.com
Search on the name of the stitch or technique you want to learn.

Pinterest
pinterest.com/LindalooEnt/
Visit my Pinterest page to view video tutorials for the stitches and techniques used in this book. Look for the board named "Amigurumi Tutorials".

Yarn

The following yarns were used for these projects.

Chef Charlotte (Worsted, #4)
    Lion Brand "Vanna's Choice": Beige, Blue & Chocolate

Chef Dress (DK, Light Worsted, #3)
    Stylecraft "Special DK": Blush & Cream

Chef Dress Variations (DK, Light Worsted, #3)

    (1) Stylecraft "Special DK": Lipstick

    (2) Stylecraft "Special DK": Fondant & Atlantis

    (3) Stylecraft "Special DK": Citron, Meadow & Spice

    (4) Stylecraft "Special DK": Lavender, Cloud Blue, Gray & Cream

Chef Uniform (DK, Light Worsted, #3)
    Stylecraft "Special DK": Candyfloss & Graphite
    Stylecraft "Batik": Graphite

Half Apron (DK, Light Worsted, #3)
    Stylecraft "Special DK": Wisteria & Fondant

Oven Mitts (DK, Light Worsted, #3)
    Stylecraft "Special DK": Storm Blue & Duck Egg

Full Apron (DK, Light Worsted, #3)
    Stylecraft "Special DK": Gray & Fondant

Cupcake Blouse (DK, Light Worsted, #3)
    Stylecraft "Special DK": Sherbet, Candyfloss, Camel & Pomegranate

Pleated Skirt (DK, Light Worsted, #3)
    Stylecraft "Special DK": Sherbet, Candyfloss, Lemon & Spring Green

Boatneck Tunic (DK, Light Worsted, #3)
    Stylecraft "Special DK": Saffron & Violet

Tulip Pants (DK, Light Worsted, #3)
    Stylecraft "Special DK": Violet

Chocolate Chip Cookie Purse (DK, Light Worsted, #3)
    Stylecraft "Special DK": Camel & Dark Brown

Confetti Donut Purse (DK, Light Worsted, #3)
    Stylecraft "Special DK": Blush & Cream

Tea Party Purse (DK, Light Worsted, #3)
    Stylecraft "Special DK": Lavender & Cream

Tea Party Hat (Worsted, #4)
    (1) Lion Brand "Vanna's Choice": Dusty Blue & Fisherman
    (2) Lion Brand "Vanna's Choice": Cranberry & Fisherman

Stole (DK, Light Worsted, #3)
    Stylecraft "Special DK": Cream

Lace Nightgown (DK, Light Worsted, #3)
    Stylecraft "Special DK": Spice

Mary Janes (DK, Light Worsted, #3)
    Stylecraft "Special DK": Tomato

Chef Shoes (DK, Light Worsted, #3)
    Stylecraft "Special DK": Black & Graphite

Sprinkle Slippers (DK, Light Worsted, #3)
    Stylecraft "Special DK": Fondant & Camel

Booties (DK, Light Worsted, #3)
    (1) Stylecraft "Special DK": Spring Green & Lemon
    (2) Stylecraft "Special DK": Gold & Cream

Tablecloth (Worsted, #4)
    Loops & Threads "Impeccable": Petunia

Tea Pot (Worsted, #4)
    Craft Smart "Value": Light Blue, Pink & Clay

Teaspoon, Fork & Knife (DK, Light Worsted, #3)
    Stylecraft "Special DK": Silver

Cream Pitcher & Sugar Bowl (Worsted, #4)
    Craft Smart "Value": Light Blue, Pink & Off White

Tea Cup & Saucer (Worsted, #4)
    Craft Smart "Value": Light Blue, Pink & Clay
  (DK, Light Worsted, #3)
    Stylecraft "Special DK": Fondant

Tea Napkin (DK, Light Worsted, #3)
    Stylecraft "Special DK": Cream & Candyfloss

Napkin Ring (Worsted, #4)
    Lion Brand "Vanna's Choice": Silver Heather

Party Plate (Worsted, #4)
    Craft Smart "Value": Cornflower, Pink & Amethyst

Serving Plate (Worsted, #4)
>(1) Craft Smart "Value": Off White
>(2) Craft Smart "Value": Light Pink

Pastry Plates (Worsted, #4)
>Craft Smart "Value": Light Pink

Vase of Flowers (Worsted, #4)
>Craft Smart "Value": Butter, Periwinkle & Leaf Green

Tea Bag (DK, Light Worsted, #3)
>Stylecraft "Special DK": Copper

Cinnamon Roll (DK, Light Worsted, #3)
>Stylecraft "Special DK": Camel & Walnut

Frosted Donut (DK, Light Worsted, #3)
>Stylecraft "Special DK": Camel & assorted colors

Macaron (DK, Light Worsted, #3)
>Stylecraft "Special DK": assorted colors

Chocolate Chip Cookie (DK, Light Worsted, #3)
>Stylecraft "Special DK": Camel

Candy Cookie (DK, Light Worsted, #3)
>Stylecraft "Special DK": Camel

Create-a-Cupcake (DK, Light Worsted, #3)
>Stylecraft "Special DK": assorted colors

Petit Fours (DK, Light Worsted, #3)
>Stylecraft "Special DK": assorted colors

Heart Sandwich Cookie (DK, Light Worsted, #3)
>Stylecraft "Special DK": Lavender & Cream

Thumbprint Cookie (DK, Light Worsted, #3)
>Stylecraft "Special DK": Camel

Rainbow Stack-a-Cake (Worsted, #4)
>Lion Brand "Vanna's Choice": White, Periwinkle, Aquamarine, Kelly Green, Terra Cotta, Pink Grapefruit
>Loops & Threads "Impeccable": Sunny Day

Chocolate Strawberry Stack-a-Cake (Worsted, #4)
>Loops & Threads "Impeccable": Chocolate & Aran
>(DK, Light Worsted, #3)
>Stylecraft "Special DK": Lipstick & Grass Green

Fruit Tart (Worsted, #4)
>Lion Brand "Vanna's Choice": Honey & Fisherman
>(DK, Light Worsted, #3)
>Stylecraft "Special DK": Lipstick, Spice, Royal, Grass Green & Spring Green

Strawberries (DK, Light Worsted, #3)
>Stylecraft "Special DK": Lipstick & Grass Green

Charlotte's Oven (Worsted, #4)
>Craft Smart "Value": Light Pink, Sage, Amethyst, & Charcoal
>Lion Brand "Vanna's Choice": Linen

Baking Sheet (Worsted, #4)
>Craft Smart "Value": Light Gray

Mixing Spoon (DK, Light Worsted, #3)
>Stylecraft "Special DK": Tomato

Lifting Spatula (DK, Light Worsted, #3)
>Stylecraft "Special DK": Storm Blue
>(Worsted, #4)
>Craft Smart "Value": Light Gray

Frosting Spatula (DK, Light Worsted, #3)
>Stylecraft "Special DK": Violet & Parchment

Mixing Bowl Worsted, #4)
>Loops & Threads "Impeccable": Fern & Aqua

Tea Towel & Pot Holder (DK, Light Worsted, #3)
>Stylecraft "Special DK": Cloud Blue & Spice

Cupcake Sleeping Bag (Worsted, #4)
>Red Heart "Super Saver": Petal Pink
>Loops & Threads "Impeccable": Sea Green, Aran, Butterscotch, Fern, Lavender & Cherry

Cookie the Cat (Worsted, #4)
>Craft Smart "Value": Off White, Black & Light Pink

Donut the Dog (Worsted, #4)
>Red Heart "Super Saver": Petal Pink, Light Raspberry & Black

Biscuit the Bear (Worsted, #4)
>Craft Smart "Value": Periwinkle, Off White & Black

Muffin the Mouse (Worsted, #4)
>Craft Smart "Value": Light Gray & Light Pink

Templates

PASTRY PLATE

UPPER TIER SUPPORT CIRCLE

Cut 1 from Corrugated Cardboard

Cut Hole

3 1/2" Diameter

PASTRY PLATE

LOWER TIER SUPPORT CIRCLE

Cut 1 from Corrugated Cardboard

Cut Hole

4 1/2" Diameter

VASE BASE

1 3/4" Diameter

Cut 1 from lightweight cardboard

Extras...just for fun!

Paper Utensil Cut-Outs

Cut page from book or make a color copy. Glue back side of sheet to printed side of cereal-box cardboard. Cover utensils with clear package tape and cut them out.

SUPPLIES
Thin cardboard (cereal box)
Glue stick
Clear package tape

Bend Spatula where handle meets blade when done.

Strawberry Charlotte Recipe

A charlotte is a dessert consisting of filling placed in a pan lined with sticks of spongecake. Kids love this version made with fluffy strawberry cream in a vessel of Twinkies®.

SUPPLIES

8" or 9" springform pan
Parchment paper
Ribbon

INGREDIENTS

1 lb. strawberries, fresh or frozen
1/2 cup white sugar
1 pkg (3 oz.) JELL-O® strawberry gelatin powder
8 oz. cream cheese
2 cups heavy whipping cream
15-18 Twinkies® cream-filled sponge cakes from 2 (15 oz.) pkgs., unwrapped

1. Thaw frozen strawberries or hull fresh strawberries. Chop into small pieces by pulsing in a food processor. Combine strawberries and sugar in a saucepan. Let sit 30 minutes, stirring occasionally.

2. Place saucepan over heat and bring to a boil. Remove from heat, add strawberry gelatin powder and stir 2 minutes until completely dissolved. Let cool to room temperature.

3. Remove cream cheese from foil wrap, place on a plate and microwave 15-20 seconds on high to soften. Transfer to a bowl and whip with electric mixer until free from lumps. Slowly add strawberry sauce and continue mixing until combined.

4. In a separate bowl, beat whipping cream until stiff peaks form. Whisk strawberry/cream cheese mixture into whipped cream in gradual increments, adding 1/4 of the amount at a time, and folding after each addition.

5. Line bottom of 8" or 9" springform pan with parchment paper. Arrange whole Twinkies® around sides of pan, standing them up as shown in picture. Cut several Twinkies® in half lengthwise and place in bottom of pan, bending them to fit. Be sure bottom is well covered. You can cut some of the Twinkies® in small pieces to fill in the gaps.

6. Pour filling into pan. If you have any excess, pour into parfait glasses for extra desserts.

7. Cover and refrigerate until firm, at least 4 hours or overnight. Decorate with a ribbon.

• •

JELL-O® is a registered trademark of Kraft Foods Group Brands LLC
Hostess® Twinkies® is a registered trademark of Hostess Brands LLC.

Chef Charlotte Coloring Page

Other Books by Linda Wright

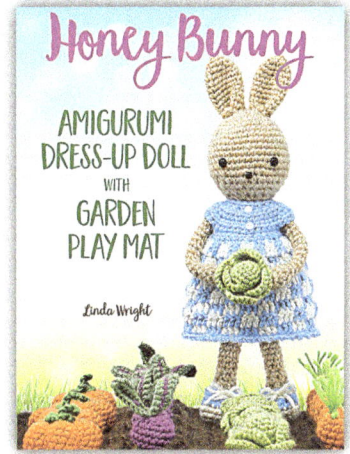
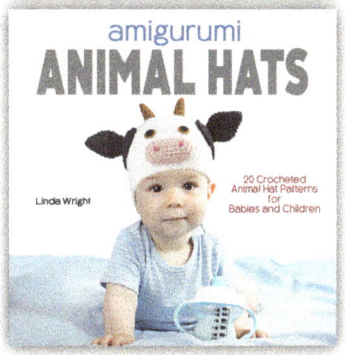
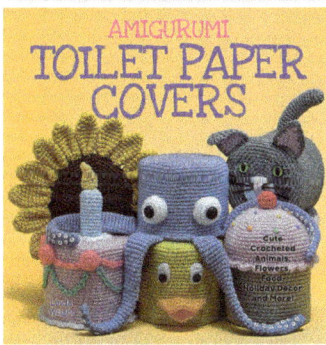

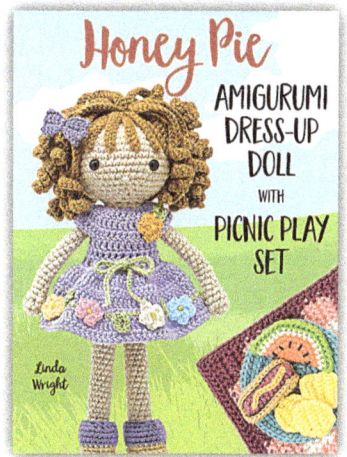

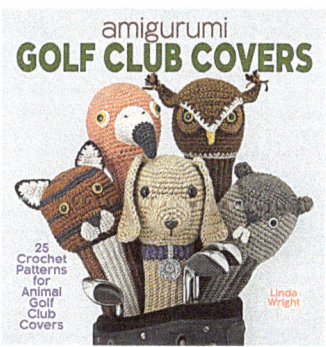

LINDA WRIGHT studied textiles, patternmaking and clothing design at the Pennsylvania State University and has had a lifelong love of creating. She is the author of various handicraft books including the groundbreaking *Toilet Paper Origami* and its companion book, *Toilet Paper Origami On a Roll*, as well as a collection of adult coloring books and numerous works of amigurumi-style crochet. To learn more about these fun-filled books, visit:

amazon.com/author/lindawright   pinterest.com/LindalooEnt   lindaloo.com

www.ingramcontent.com/pod-product-compliance
Lightning Source LLC
Chambersburg PA
CBHW060921170426
43191CB00024B/2450